D0451179

The Making of a Teacher

The

MAKING

of a

TEACHER

Conversations with

EKNATH

EASWARAN

by Tim & Carol Flinders

Nilgiri Press

First printing February 1989

The Blue Mountain Center of Meditation, founded in Berkeley in 1960
by Eknath Easwaran, publishes books on how to lead the spiritual life
in the home and the community. For information please write to
Nilgiri Press, Box 477, Petaluma, California 94953.

Library of Congress Cataloging–in–Publication Data:

Flinders, Tim.
    The making of a teacher : conversations with Eknath Easwaran
by Tim & Carol Flinders.
        p.   cm.
    ISBN 0–915132–55–9 : $22.00.
    ISBN 0–915132–54–0 (pbk.) : $12.00.
    1. Easwaran, Eknath.   2. Religious biography.   3. Spiritual life.
I. Flinders, Carol.   II. Easwaran, Eknath.   III. Title.
    BL73.E18F57 1989
    294.5'512'0924 — dc19   88–3467
    [B]   CIP

Table of Contents

Foreword

Eknath Easwaran has been a teacher of meditation in this country for more than a quarter of a century. Tens of thousands have heard him speak since he founded the Blue Mountain Center of Meditation, and more than a quarter of a million copies of his books on meditation and the spiritual life are in print. People read his books and practice his teachings in many countries around the world, and his meditation retreats draw enthusiastic seekers from every region of the United States.

For a great many of the people whose lives have been touched by Easwaran, it isn't enough just to know that there *is* such a man. "*Who* is he?" they ask, through letters, at retreats, and at his Tuesday night talks. "What is he really like? And how did he get to be that way?" Rarely are these questions posed out of simple curiosity. They spring, rather, from the same source as those questions that bring one to pick up a book on meditation in the first place, or to go to a meditation retreat or a talk on the spiritual life: "Who am I? What am I really like? And how can I become what I want to be?"

For several years I had been keeping notes for a book I hoped might help answer some of those questions about Easwaran. More than a year ago, I gave him a manuscript. He read it and declared it "a good foundation," but said there was much more he would like the book to convey. He suggested, to begin with, that my wife, Carol, lend a helping hand. "Particularly where it comes to my granny and my village," he said, "there are things that a woman can best observe and describe." The timing was right. Carol had just finished more than a decade of food writing and was more than happy to be drawn into the work. What began as "a helping hand" evolved over the ensuing months into a wonderfully congenial collaboration.

Our aim has been to trace Easwaran's development as a spiritual teacher – as much as possible, in his own words. Thus, our conversations with him form the heart of the book. It is not intended to be read as a biography or a memoir. Perhaps it can best be approached as oral history. We have tried to set forth what Easwaran said and to convey some feeling of what it's like to be with him when he's talking. To that end, we have edited the conversations for readability and arranged them to follow the chronology of Easwaran's spiritual development. In some cases, several conversations have been combined to form a single chapter. Many of the names used in the text are pseudonyms: guests at Easwaran's retreats feel comfortable speaking openly about themselves, and we'd like them to go on feeling that way!

A brief summary of the events pertinent to this book might be helpful in following the conversations.

Born into an ancient and traditional family in a beauti-

ful village in South India, Eknath Easwaran (pronounced
Ish-war-an) was brought up by his mother and by *her*
mother in the midst of a large extended family. He was
particularly close to his grandmother, but it wasn't until
much later that he realized that she was his spiritual
teacher.

Easwaran was schooled in his village until he was sixteen, when he left home to attend a Catholic college fifty
miles away. After receiving a bachelor's degree in English
literature, he went on to do graduate work at the University of Nagpur, receiving degrees with honors in both English and law. A teaching appointment at a small college
in central India followed. Before long, Easwaran was also
gaining a reputation as a writer and public speaker. Later,
he returned to the University of Nagpur as chairman of
the Department of English.

Easwaran's work in this country began with his arrival
here on a Fulbright fellowship in 1959. He gave meditation
talks throughout the San Francisco Bay Area, and it was at
one of these talks that he met Christine, who later became
his wife. She has played a central role in his work and
helped him found the Blue Mountain Center of Meditation
in Berkeley in 1961. A four-year stay in India followed.

Easwaran returned to the Bay Area in December of 1965
and resumed the teaching of meditation. Throughout the
late 1960s his audience grew rapidly, and in 1970 he established Ramagiri Ashram, a spiritual community composed
of a core group of dedicated meditation students. The following years have been spent developing the community,
writing numerous books about meditation and the spiritual life, and continuing his weekly public talks.

Here and throughout the book we have sketched in
some of the external events that have affected Easwaran's
development as a spiritual teacher, but the real topic of
this book is an *inner* transformation, which occurred

gradually over decades. When Easwaran tells his story, he divides it into three sequential periods; we have treated each, respectively, in our second, third, and fourth chapters.

The first chapter is set at one of the Blue Mountain Center's meditation retreats. We have attempted here to give a vivid rendering of how Easwaran teaches and to provide the background information necessary for understanding the conversations which follow.

The second chapter revolves around a morning conversation at Easwaran's spiritual community during which he describes his childhood – the years before he went away to college, when his spiritual teacher, his grandmother, laid the foundations for what was to come.

In the third chapter, during a long walk on a beach near the ashram, Easwaran talks about his college years and professional achievements – but more to the point, about the spiritual crisis that plunged him into a search for the fulfillment he hadn't found.

An afternoon trip to Berkeley forms the backdrop for the fourth chapter, as Easwaran recounts the dramatic course of events that led him to turn inward, to develop his method of meditation, and then, in the climax of meditation, to find the enduring source of fulfillment he had been seeking.

The fifth chapter takes place at a Tuesday night talk and tries to convey what all of us around him now are seeing: a man at the peak of his powers – more eloquent, more outward-looking, and more buoyant than ever.

This book began as my effort – became *our* effort when Carol joined me – to render some kind of portrait of Easwaran. But it has ended up being very much

Easwaran's own effort too. When he told us there was more that he wanted the book to convey, we wondered what that "more" was and how he would communicate it to us.

We didn't have to wait long. The next morning, he launched a series of extended conversations during which several of his friends were encouraged to question him closely about his life, particularly about his development as a spiritual teacher. "What was *your* teacher like? How did she teach you? And how have *you* become what you are?" For many years we had asked him questions like these, and his answers had always been inspiring and empowering; but now they took on new depth and detail. These were unforgettable sessions, laced with laughter and poignancy and, sometimes, sheer wonder. They lifted the book to a new level. At the heart of it all – what became the *leitmotif* of the book itself – was his relationship with his teacher, his grandmother.

This procedure was entirely in keeping with what Easwaran says about the relationship between teacher and student. Whatever a teacher possesses of wisdom, love, and insight, he says, can only be *drawn* out by the student's deep and focused desire to know, to love, and to understand. Indeed, an almost electric atmosphere surrounds Easwaran when he is with people who have that kind of desire, and in this book we have tried to recreate that atmosphere. But the men and women who are close at hand –at Tuesday night talks, at retreats, or in his community – are by no means the only ones who exert this powerful tug on Easwaran. The needs of a much greater number press in on him with real force. This group includes people who practice meditation along his lines but cannot see or hear him regularly. It includes, for that matter, everyone who has ever felt the need to ask those perennial questions: "Who am I? What am I really like? How can I become what I want to be?"

That Easwaran has played so active a role in bringing out this book is in part a tribute to all these individuals and to the intensity of *their* desire for spiritual awareness.

At a retreat, 1988

At a retreat, 1988

Christine Easwaran

With Christine

1 | Santa Sabina
Profile of a Teacher

A young couple from Maine were the first to register. They were distributors of organic produce, they told us, who had found one of Easwaran's books in their local bookstore. They had begun to meditate, then had written to Nilgiri Press for a catalog and learned in that way about these weekend retreats. Shortly after them, at two-thirty, a college student from Austin, Texas, arrived – an alumnus, he reminded us, grinning broadly. This was his second visit. He stowed his backpack, then went off to the swimming pool with a towel over his shoulder. At three o'clock a retired businessman from Minnesota drove in with his wife; he had given her this trip to the retreat as an anniversary gift.

Official registration time for the retreats is four o'clock on Friday afternoon. But the first guests have usually arrived by two, while some invariably pull in as late as dinnertime. The spread is understandable, for people are coming from great distances.

On this particular August evening, most of the rooms in

the Santa Sabina Center had been claimed by six o'clock, and the guests were having dinner at small tables set up on the lawn behind the conference room. It was still daylight, but Santa Sabina was lapped in its own partial twilight: the sun had already dropped behind a line of tall eucalyptus trees. To the north and east of the center stands a steep bluff, part of the Dominican College compus, where Santa Sabina is located. Covered with eucalyptus trees and left undeveloped except for fire trails, the hill forms a natural buffer between the campus and the urban sprawl that lies just beyond. A grove of deciduous trees mixed with fir and redwood marks the northern rim of the retreat center. Sitting here now, one felt almost encircled by forest, and it was hard to believe that San Francisco was only twenty-five minutes away. The lengthening shadows were welcome, for the day had been hot.

In all, seventy-five people had enrolled for the retreat. Carol and I had been here with several others most of the afternoon, helping people settle in, showing them where the walking paths start up the hill, getting reacquainted with guests like our young friend from Texas: thirty-five of the registrants had been here at least once before.

Wherever you looked after dinner, small knots of people sat or stood, talking animatedly. A woman from North Carolina and another from Arizona who had been roommates at a former retreat were chatting as if at a class reunion. By the volleyball net on the far side of the lawn, half a dozen college students were carrying on their own parley.

The professional diversity of the people attending these retreats has been as broad as the geographic spread, and this one was no exception. Sitting with us at dinner were, an emergency room physician, a house painter, a therapist, and a woman who runs a day-care center out of her home. A journalist was there too – a young woman who had

begun to meditate when the profession she had hoped
would be "a mission" in life turned out to be, finally, "just
a job." Her energy and idealism were still running strong,
she told us, and she hoped meditation would help her re-
direct them. Three physicians had enrolled, and several
teachers.

A certain ebullience could be felt – more than that, an
air of anticipation. These people had not flown in from
Florida, Oregon, and New Mexico for a relaxing weekend;
they had come to see and hear the man whose books they
had been reading for months, or years, and to draw what
they could from his presence.

And he would not keep them waiting. Easwaran has
never been one for dramatic entrances. His talk was
scheduled for seven-thirty, but he was already moving
easily among the guests before dinner was over. He and his
wife, Christine, greeted returnees, chatted in the kitchen
with the caterer and her staff, and had some of us bring
newcomers to him to be introduced: a retired college professor, among others, and a Catholic priest whose ministry
is devoted to people affected by AIDS. Some of the time he
spent just walking about quietly, observing, perhaps listening, getting a sense of the audience he was about to
address.

By 7:20 the courtyard and dining room had emptied
and everyone had taken a seat in the rows of chairs and
couches that spanned the length of the conference room.
Easwaran sat down in an armchair on a raised platform at
the front. On a small table next to him was a blue por-
celain cup of herbal tea – he would be sipping from it
throughout his talk to protect his throat – and a bright
cloth napkin. There were no notes. After almost three decades of introducing meditation to American audiences,
Easwaran hardly needed to recall the ground he was about
to cover.

Chapter One

Shifting in his chair, he turned to his left, his gaze sweeping over the line of faces that curved in a shallow semicircle to the far wall. A slight breeze off nearby San Francisco Bay drifted through the room. Conversations trailed off. Programs were set down; the gathering grew quiet.

The sound man clipped a microphone to Easwaran's lapel. I was to introduce him that evening and was looking for the nod that would signal me to begin. Watching him as I waited, I found myself wondering what it would be like to be seeing him now for the first time, as many of these people were. Twenty years ago, the clarity and vigor of his features had dazzled me – dazzled everyone, I think, who met him. Today, in his mid-seventies, the cinematic good looks are tempered but hardly less arresting. The tawny luster of his face and skin are lit now by pearl white at the temples and by a closely cropped white mustache. The soft gray flannel Indian suit he was wearing tonight matched the ever-present beret, worn aslant. The sheen of the face and hands and the soft, lively gaze belied his years. He seemed ageless, I was thinking, out of time altogether.

The nod came. I stood up, thinking I had a fair idea of what I wanted to say by way of introduction. But one look at the gathering changed my mind. Between him and his audience there was already such depth of feeling, and such absolute readiness, that my prepared remarks were surely best set aside. "It gives me great pleasure," I said, "to introduce Eknath Easwaran."

He looked out again into the audience, gave a glance to a familiar face, then smiled suddenly toward the back of the room and waved.

Five college students had just finished dinner cleanup and were now trying inconspicuously to find seats. Easwaran leaned forward in his chair and beckoned them to the open space on the carpet in front of him. Cheered, if a little self-conscious, they hurried forward, picking up cushions from unoccupied couches. While they made their way to the front, Easwaran spotted a few other young people already seated and waved them closer too.

He paused for a moment as they settled in, folding their legs underneath them and pulling themselves upright. Then, lifting his gaze to a point far past the last row, he began to speak about . . . *mountain climbing,* though as far as I knew there was not a single mountaineer among us.

"In the long crescent of mountains ranging from Pakistan to Nepal, from the Karakorams to the Himalayas, stand fourteen towering peaks. Experienced climbers call them 'eight-thousanders' because each rises past the height of eight thousand meters – more than twenty-six thousand feet – above sea level." He spoke deliberately, each word distinct and significant. A twenty-five-year immersion in American casualness has hardly touched the rounded, formal vowels first learned in British India.

"From the human standpoint, that height is critical. Above the altitude of eight thousand meters, a physical curtain falls, and most ordinary human beings can climb no higher without the assistance of special equipment. There are, however, a few men and women, dauntless and determined, who are prepared to make these difficult ascents without any equipment.

"Recently, an Italian climber named Reinhold Messner announced that he had climbed all the fourteen peaks without any equipment, not even oxygen. At those altitudes the air becomes so rarefied that it is almost impossible to breathe, and the average person cannot last long without portable oxygen. But Reinhold Messner is not average. He has the capacity to breathe more quickly as the air gets thinner, and – more significantly – he has what his friends call 'creative innovation,' the 'extra imagi-

Chapter One

native drive' to accomplish a feat that has long been considered impossible."

If the audience was puzzled by the talk's direction, I could see no signs of it. This was a meditation retreat, and Easwaran is a teacher of meditation, but these were people who knew his books. They could see where he was heading.

Easwaran's fascination with mountaineering comes from the drive and dedication it demands, the single-minded sense of purpose that, he points out, is essential to success in meditation. Although he has a deep and genuine admiration for climbers like Reinhold Messner, Easwaran's books make it clear that the mountains which truly command his attention are not to be found among the Himalayas or the Karakorams or any other range, East or West. They are to be found within, rising from the vast and fearful terrain of human consciousness.

"Messner travels light," he told the audience. "He takes only the minimum equipment and supplies he needs to survive at those elevations. For the most part, he relies only on his own resourcefulness. When someone asked Messner for the secret of his success, he gave a revealing reply. It was *desire,* the irresistible urge to climb each of the fourteen eight-thousanders alone and unaided.

"*That* is his real genius. More than anything else, it was this single-mindedness that enabled Messner to do what no other climber has been able to do: not just to survive at those unimaginable heights but actually to *thrive* there, whether it was K2 or Kanchenjunga that he was climbing."

Easwaran cleared his throat and took two sips of herbal tea. He set the cup down carefully and balanced the still-folded napkin atop it to hold in the heat.

"I am deeply drawn to people like Reinhold Messner,"

he said, his voice soft and resonant, "people who dare and are not content to follow the petty, predictable urges of life, people who travel light and do not let themselves become needlessly encumbered. In every walk of life, people who unify their desires go far; those who travel light climb high."

Sitting cross-legged on the floor just in front of Easwaran was a compact, wiry young man with the high forehead and delicate features of a Florentine youth – the kind Botticelli might have painted, only dressed in faded jeans and a yellow T-shirt. Almost imperceptibly, at Easwaran's last words he pulled himself upright and gathered in his breath.

"Every age has produced a few rare men and women who find the pursuit of pleasure and profit too constricting. Such people will never be satisfied merely playing with life's toys. They have an urgent need to live at higher elevations, in the loftiest regions of human consciousness."

Saint Francis of Assisi, Teresa of Avila, the nineteenth-century Bengali saint Sri Ramakrishna, Mahatma Gandhi: these, he said, were "magnificent creatures" who lived at the very summit of human consciousness. "Each of these courageous adventurers discovered that life lived at the highest reaches of consciousness brings unending joy and fulfillment. And they all made the claim that we too can join them, if we want.

"Twenty-five hundred years ago in ancient India, one of these adventurers, the Compassionate Buddha, likened the experience of reaching life's summit to waking up from a dream. The Buddha taught that compared with our tremendous capacity for awareness, for compassion and love, we are all asleep, dreaming that we can be satisfied by a few physical pleasures, or by fame or power."

Few people believed the Buddha then, Easwaran said,

and probably fewer still would believe him today. "'Oh no, Blessed One,' we would tell him, 'we are awake! We can tell.'

"I know," he added with a smile. "I was like that too. In those days, I was a successful professor. I loved my work and was passionately fond of my students. I was not bored or depressed or insecure. I enjoyed art and literature and music. I *had* to be awake.

"And yet," he said, suddenly serious, "all of that was not enough. It was only when I took to meditation, and began to discover the immense treasure house of joy and wisdom within, that I realized that I had indeed been asleep. With respect to my deepest capacities, I had been asleep – dreaming – and getting paid for it! Had it not been for my grandmother's blessing, I undoubtedly would have lived out my life in this dream – teaching, writing, enjoying the innocent pleasures of life – just like the millions the Buddha talked of, the millions who are born, grow up, go to school, have careers, raise families, and pass away without ever discovering who they are.

"I never really began to live, never really woke up, until I began to meditate and started to climb some of these eight-thousanders within the mind. That is the purpose of meditation," he said emphatically: "to enable every person to wake up and find the answers to the questions that stir in the depths of consciousness: Who am I? What am I here for?

"Let me assure you, it's not easy. But any man or woman can do it. What it takes is daring, determination, complete dedication, and . . . patience." He removed the napkin and picked up his cup. "You will need the patience of a person trying to empty the sea with a little cup like this. It may take decades of driving inward, years of climbing upward to find the answers, but in this country, which is noted for its drive and enthusiasm, I have no doubt that there are thousands of people who are capable of this great adventure." He put down the cup and, with a sweep of his hand, pointed to the young students crowded on the floor in front of him. "Messners in the making. All that I have said so far, all I will say throughout this retreat, all that my books are about, is *what it means to wake up.*"

2 |

Eknath Easwaran comes from an ancient, well-landed, aristocratic family in Kerala state, South India, home of the coconut palm and a deeply rooted Hindu orthodoxy. His village is relatively large (with about three thousand inhabitants), prosperous, slow paced, and beautiful. Easwaran's ancestors were a martial clan – their long, curved swords still hang in the ancestral home. Local legend has it that in return for loyal service, a maharaja offered them an ample portion of his lands, "as much as you can see." As it happened, one family member had "the eyes of an eagle." He went to work and traced out a vast parcel indeed.

When he was a boy, Easwaran lived in the Eknath manor house, in the midst of a large extended family of aunts, cousins, and uncles of all ages and temperaments. The family was well-to-do but lived simply. One regular and unquestioned extravagance was to bring in a caparisoned elephant or two for religious festivals. In fact, the main gate of the family compound was arched especially high to permit easy entry for elephants.

In Kerala, women have had full legal rights for centuries. Nowhere in India have women a higher degree of literacy, and a strong section of Hindu society in Kerala is still matrilineal: the lineage is traced through the womenfolk. The Eknaths are one of these. Easwaran's family name, Eknath, comes to him through his mother and through her mother, Easwaran's maternal grandmother, the primary influence in his life. (His given name, Easwaran, was a gift from his grandmother. One of the many Hindu names for God, it means "He who rules from within.") "Big Granny" to the village, a person of towering spiritual capacities, Easwaran's grandmother was to him a companion, counselor, refuge, and playmate. In time, he would come to regard her as his spiritual teacher.

At sixteen, he left the village to study at a small Catholic college fifty miles from his home. He would have been a natural for Oxford, and his teachers wanted him to go there, but his family's finances had become too strained by then to permit that. As it turned out, he had fine teachers at the Catholic college and grew particularly close to the principal, a Kerala priest who had been trained in Edinburgh. Easwaran's great passion – to the expense of his other subjects – was English literature. After earning higher degrees in English and law, he became an instructor of English literature at a small college. He began to publish fiction, writing in English, and later became chairman of the English department of a major Indian university. There seemed to be no reason why he should not look forward to a productive campus life and writing career, "lost in the world of literature."

Then, without warning, that boundless world became "a prison-house." A terrible restlessness overtook him. He tried to find release in work, in recreation, in relationships, in literature and the arts – and they all failed him. When he had exhausted every other avenue, he turned inward and began to meditate and to alter his life, as he puts it, "in a hundred different ways."

So far, the pattern of Easwaran's life holds true to one that is well documented in India's ancient spiritual tradition; had it continued to hold true, Easwaran might have withdrawn soon afterward from professional life – disappeared, perhaps, and turned up years later in a monastery or a mountain cave, or in one of the holy cities like Benares or Vrindavan, to live out his days in meditation and study of the scriptures.

Instead, Easwaran stayed at the university. Into an already taxing schedule of writing, teaching, and administrative duties he worked one hour, then two, then, finally, four hours of meditation a day. It was his grandmother's example, he explains, that persuaded him that intense spiritual disciplines could be followed in the midst of an active, engaged life. "This was her way," he has said. "She always lived among us."

His progress was rapid, even by Indian standards. An innate talent for meditation quickly drew him within to a depth that both astonished and alarmed him, as well as the people to whom he went for guidance. They could not help him. Forced to rely solely on his own resources, he realized that although his grandmother had already "shed her body," he was not alone. "She had done all the essential work," he has said, "by the time I left for college." Prepared by her for some of the profoundest inner experiences on the spiritual journey, he neared its goal filled with disbelief at his progress and at his grandmother's "incalculable grace."

Of the depths he touched in meditation, only Easwaran can speak, and he is by temperament averse to discussing them openly. In carefully guarded terms he will say, describing life as it once appeared to him, "It was not unreal, but I can see now that it had only a limited, partial reality. Then I saw the world; now I see *into* the world. I see the Self, the divine spirit that throbs at the heart of every creature."

A few of the people around him, sensing something, sought his guidance. Indians are not slow to perceive spiritual awareness, even when it appears in the unlikely garb of a properly bookish, unassuming English professor. And in a quiet way, he did provide guidance for a few. But it would be a long time before he would think of himself as a spiritual teacher or permit anyone else to. That role, with its daunting responsibilities, he neither relished nor sought.

It was as a visiting scholar on a Fulbright fellowship that Easwaran first traveled to the United States in 1959. Although he had already begun to change his professional interests – in his words, "from education for degrees to education for living" – it would be inaccurate to say that he saw his future spiritual work clearly laid out. Yet it would be almost as inaccurate to say that he did not. There were glimmerings, and a strong hunch. There was his background in teaching. But most of all, there was his driving need to share his discovery with the students he loved. Carefully assessing the atmosphere in this country, he listened, watched, and made some educated guesses.

One private college in Minnesota made him an attractive offer: he could have full charge of a fledgling India Studies program, developing it as he saw fit. He declined. Something was guiding him elsewhere, wordlessly, like the needle of a compass. Whatever he was moving toward, he was certain it was nothing so decidedly academic.

Yet for all practical purposes, he proceeded as if he were still a wholehearted professional academic. When he pressed the State Department for a reassignment, it wasn't just because the subzero Minnesota weather was more than he had bargained for; he had a sound scholarly motive. The subject he had come to the United States to investigate was the influence of the Upanishads, India's most venerable mystical texts, on Ralph Waldo Emerson. There was a professor at the University of California at Berkeley who was an authority on Emerson and had a keen interest in the Eastern roots of transcendentalism.

And so he went to Berkeley, looking forward to active

participation in U.C.'s English department. But he did have more than Emerson on his mind.

In Kansas the students had endeared themselves to him with their freshness, and in Minneapolis he had found some who asked probing questions. But he hadn't found the inner fire, the responsive light in the eye that something told him he was looking for. He would describe later the kind of student he was half-consciously seeking: "bright, sophisticated, with just a little wickedness, and ready to test the limits of conventional wisdom." Maybe he would find that fire in California.

And indeed he did, though not at first in university students. It would be another five years before the free speech movement made Berkeley the epicenter of the youth movement that jolted Western culture, and in 1960, even in Berkeley, spiritual restlessness was still as dormant as political dissidence.

People came, though, to listen to Easwaran read and comment on the Upanishads and, after the talks, to meditate with him. Soon he was giving talks five nights a week and leading a long meditation on a sixth night. It was a diverse group from many walks of life (including a fair number of beatniks), multiracial, enthusiastic, and very hospitable. Many opened their homes to him.

Among those who came and stayed was Christine, who had arrived in the Bay Area the same month he had. Together they founded the Blue Mountain Center of Meditation in 1961, but soon the terms of the Fulbright fellowship obliged Easwaran to return to India.

In December of 1965, he and Christine were back in Berkeley, a city that had soared to international prominence during his absence. A revolution in thought and attitude among the young had begun, and its focal point, the crucible, was Berkeley. Even serious, middle-class students were dropping out of school, experimenting with mind-altering drugs, and wearing flowers in hair that was considerably longer than it had been in 1961. Some of the most thoughtful of those who had challenged the authority of school and state were now ready to take that same questioning inward, and Easwaran was eager to assist them. "Rebelling against oppressive political structures, well and good," he told them, "but only the truly courageous can rebel against what is selfish and separate within themselves."

Not long after his return, Easwaran began offering regular talks at his home in Oakland, and eventually on the campus itself. The talks were free, just as they had been before his departure to India. He was determined to build the Center on freewill donations, a practice entirely in keeping with the Indian spiritual tradition. Since he had resigned his professorship in India, though, and returned to the United States with no assured means of financial support, finances had become precarious in the extreme. He would have to make his own way, depending on the good will of those who came to hear him speak, and that was how he wanted it.

He would not charge for his talks, nor would he advertise them. He felt sure that word of mouth communication would attract a more earnest and committed following. In the spiritual hothouse of the Bay Area during the mid-sixties, word spread quickly and his audiences grew. When the Oakland home could no longer accommodate the increased attendance, Easwaran and Christine moved the talks to a larger site in Berkeley, just a few blocks from the campus. Within a few years the BMCM had grown into a flourishing center for people committed to shaping their lives around the practice of meditation. The most dedicated students would eventually require close, daily guidance, Easwaran knew. So, in 1970, he and Christine moved to a property in rural Marin County that earlier had

served as a dairy ranch, then a small Catholic seminary.
It was there that he established his spiritual community,
commuting to Berkeley for public talks until 1977, when
they were moved to a church in Petaluma. These talks,
which he continues to give every Tuesday night, are – like
the hundreds he gave in Oakland and Berkeley during the
sixties and the thousands that have followed – still free.

Three years ago, Easwaran decided to offer overnight meditation retreats for the first time, and he spent considerable
time looking into the facilities available just north of San
Francisco. None quite measured up: that one was too rus-
tic, this one too remote from public transportation. But
when he walked into Santa Sabina, his search was over.
The calm of the place impressed him immediately. So did
the warmth and kindliness of the Dominican sisters who
run the center as their vocation.

Santa Sabina Center has been a retreat facility for seven-
teen years, yet it still retains something of the conventual
atmosphere. Patterned after the traditional medieval clois-
ter – insular, calming, intense – its tranquility enters your
blood soon after you arrive, and lingers there surprisingly
long after you leave.

Santa Sabina was built during the 1930s as a novitiate
for the order of Saint Dominic. Its proportions are gener-
ous: a large two-story quadrangle encloses a courtyard
with a sheltered walkway and garden and, alongside it,
a long, sunny conference room.

There is room to stroll about, places where it's a pleasure just to sit quietly; places, too, that invite settling in
for conversation. The arched walkways are cool and dim,
but light spills into the library, tumbles into the open
courtyard, and pours through the high, leaded window-
panes of a chapel that is all the more arresting for its simplicity: no stained glass, just a glimpse of silver-green

eucalyptus tossing against a blue sky. With the tiled hall-
ways, the formal chapel, and, most of all, the alluring, mo-
bile light, Saint Catherine of Siena would have felt at
home here.

Easwaran certainly does. For him there is no contradic-
tion, any more than there was for Catherine, between a
life of contemplation and a life of action. As he often reminds his audiences, it is entirely possible to lead an active, ardent spiritual life right in the midst of the modern
world, working hard, living with family and friends, yet all
the while maintaining the calm detachment and dedication of a solitary monastic.

Easwaran calls himself a "practical idealist." Spiritual
awareness, he points out, reveals itself as eloquently in
character development and selfless action as in mystical
states. "God reveals Himself in action," he likes to say;
authentic mystical experience changes the way you see
the world and the way you live. "If you want to judge your
progress," he says, "ask yourself these questions: Are you
more loving? Is your judgment sounder? Do you have
more energy? Can your mind remain calm under provoca-
tion? Are you free from the conditioning of anger, fear, and
greed?"

Easwaran's eight-point program is pragmatic and sweeping: meditation; the silent repetition of a mantram, or
holy name; slowing down; one-pointed attention; training
the senses; putting others first; spiritual reading; and *satsang,* or spiritual fellowship.

Meditation is anything but easy. "It may require a lifetime to master," he cheerily tells his audiences, "but it
will have been a lifetime well spent. Those who offer instant enlightenment mislead us. After all, we have to
bring the mind itself under control, and there is no more
difficult task in life. My form of meditation is for those

who are prepared for a lifetime of challenge. But then, we need challenges, or we stagnate."

He speaks from experience. "I *love* challenges," he says. And he goes to great lengths, it appears to many of his close associates, to ensure that he has an ample supply of them. "To me, lack of stress is *dis*tress," he tells us. "I wouldn't know what to do without challenges." At an age when most people would have retired happily from active life, he has launched a long-term project for people affected by life-threatening illness, especially HIV infection. The project is currently called the RISE program. Easwaran acts as the meditation consultant to RISE classes, which are offered in several locations throughout the country. A manual has been published that adapts his eight points to a health program. Now, he says, he wants his students to design a research project to document the benefits he is certain the program can bring to persons affected by most life-threatening illnesses.

Responding to the AIDS crisis was not the departure for Easwaran that it might appear. Since the BMCM's incorporation as a nonprofit educational organization, he has sought to make meditation known as a tool for promoting human welfare and relieving suffering. His interests have ranged over a broad spectrum of human concerns that include health, education, family life, and peace. His RISE program is only the latest in a series of medical projects.

Fundamental to the growth of Easwaran's work has been the steady success of the Center's publishing arm. Started with a multilith press in a leaky garage, it has developed, under Christine's supervision, into a highly respected small press. Nilgiri Press has more than a quarter of a million copies in print of over a dozen books by Easwaran on meditation, spiritual living, and nonviolence, including a popular biography of Mahatma Gandhi and a series of translations, with commentary, of India's spiritual classics. It also published the best-selling vegetarian cookbook *Laurel's Kitchen*, written by some of his students.

In addition to his books, Easwaran contributes occasional articles to the *Christian Science Monitor* and to journals such as *Parabola*. Interviews with him have appeared in a variety of publications, among them the *East West Journal*, *The Benedictine* magazine, the *Los Angeles Times*, and *The New Yorker*. One of his students has founded a peace studies program at the University of California; others have established a small private school at the ashram with a curriculum based on spiritual values. Still others are engaged in a project to save the elephant, in danger today in Africa as well as Asia.

"Once someone told me that I live five thousand years in the past," Easwaran has said, referring to his persistent campaigns to relieve suffering. "He was half right, since there is strong evidence that the Indian mystical tradition I represent may well be that old. Certainly it is at least thirty-five hundred years old. But I told this person that I also live five thousand years in the future. For the problem that this tradition addresses – the issue of human suffering – will be as vital to people five thousand years from now as it was to my forebears, as it is now."

Responding to the needs of others is not a burden or even a matter of philanthropy for the mystic, according to Easwaran. When a man or woman wakes up to the unity which underlies all of life, he says, selfless action becomes as natural, and as necessary, as breathing: "Those who attain Self-realization can live afterward in the sea of change without being swept away. They live only to give, and their capacity to go on giving is a source of joy so great that it cannot be measured against any sensation the world offers."

3

The shy young Hispanic woman from California's Central Valley smiled bravely from her chair and told Easwaran that nothing could have kept her from attending this retreat. She had held a garage sale, she said, to finance the trip. Her car had broken down on the way, but passing strangers had lent a hand, and here she was. "Must have been fated," she said, giggling.

It was Saturday evening at Santa Sabina. Everyone was gathered in the conference room for evening *satsang*, spiritual fellowship, with Easwaran.

It had been a full day. In the morning, small group sessions had discussed Easwaran's eight-point spiritual program. After lunch, some of his students had described different phases of the Center's work. The authors of *The New Laurel's Kitchen* answered questions about vegetarianism: What if your husband doesn't . . . ? ("Don't pressure him.") Do you recommend honey over brown sugar? ("Sugar is sugar is sugar. Keep the bees employed.") Another group had followed with a report on their work with the RISE program. Then a group of young people from the Center's small school had taken turns describing the wildlife club they had formed.

Friends of Wildlife (FOWL) had already worked for a few years to protect endangered species, the children had told the audience, and were now trying to raise two thousand dollars to enable Masai tribesmen in Kenya to build an electric fence. The fence would ward off roving elephants who were destroying seventy-five percent of the tribe's crops. It was a mutually congenial solution to a knotty problem, protecting the crops as well as the elephants that were being speared (thirty each year) by the tribesmen. FOWL had already raised seven hundred and fifty dollars by selling T-shirts and a handsome poster.

Chapter One

After the talks there had been a volleyball game, walks, swimming, reading in the library, and much conversation. Dinner in the refectory would have laid to rest any lingering fears that a vegetarian diet is inherently meager: lasagna, whole wheat sourdough bread, steamed green beans with lemon butter, a garden salad with sesame dressing, and, if you were still unconvinced, apple crisp made with early Gravensteins and topped with yogurt. The decibel level of eighty or so retreatants getting to know each other exceeded what you might have expected in a convent refectory, but no one seemed to mind.

And now, satsang.

Easwaran asked that the introductions begin from the end chair in the front row, with the shy young woman from Fresno. She had three children, she told us, and though she had been meditating only a year, it had changed her life – especially, it had developed her capacities as a mother. Seeing Easwaran in person meant a great deal to her, she said. Somehow or other, she would manage to attend more retreats in the future. "There are still some things left in the garage."

A second young woman introduced herself. Sounding as if she were close to tears, she told how meditation had made it possible for her to help – and to love – an alcoholic father.

A reserved, plainspoken man from the South explained that he had been a seeker for several years but had long been "leery" of spiritual groups, "with what you read in the papers and all." He had been reading Easwaran's books for some time and was especially struck by their sanity and common sense. He decided to come out and see what it was all about. "So far," he added, sitting back down, "I like what I see."

A soft-spoken lawyer from southern California said that

he had attended an earlier retreat and was just glad to be there. "It feels like coming home."

Sometimes Easwaran nodded or smiled. Saying little himself, he met each individual with a level of attention that seemed almost tangible. If he couldn't see a speaker's face, he shifted himself to the side of his chair or asked if the speaker would slide into view. Throughout the satsang, each person who spoke with him became engaged in a visual dialogue of such intensity that it felt at times as if no one else were in the room.

The next person smiled when it was her turn to speak, but remained silent. "Go ahead," Easwaran encouraged with a grin. Christine Easwaran looked back at him, her blue-gray eyes alight, but said nothing.

"This is my wife, Christine," Easwaran said. "Christine is from Virginia. We are both southerners."

Christine Easwaran has been a prominent force in the work and life of the Blue Mountain Center since its inception. Her touch is most visible in the deliberate manner in which the Center has progressed, in the congenial, ordered life of the ashram, and especially in the character and development of Nilgiri Press. "Christine has been with me since the beginning of this work twenty-five years ago," Easwaran said. "I could not have carried it on without her."

A sturdy man with a brown beard and deep, wide-set eyes spoke next. "I've been meditating for two years now," he said. "It has not been easy for me. There are times when I find it too difficult to go on meditating, and then I stop." He paused as the audience took in what he said. Several people nodded, identifying with his struggle. Then he added, "But I find it even more difficult *not* to go on meditating." More nods, and a ripple of sympathetic laughter.

Chapter One

The next speaker, a tall man with a rugged face, talked in a wry, clipped accent about his struggle with drug abuse. His wife, sitting next to him, said that the inspiration they had drawn from Easwaran's books had saved their family.

Down the row from them, a nun explained that she had become interested in Easwaran for two reasons, the first being their shared interest in Gandhi. The second was the Better Butter recipe from *Laurel's Kitchen.* There were a few smiles at the incongruity, but she was not the first, nor the last, who had become interested in Easwaran and meditation through the popular vegetarian cookbook.

Easwaran nodded and looked toward the next speaker, a middle-aged man who spoke with deliberate articulation. He gave his name and added, without emotion, "Four years ago, my life came to an end."

He paused. "I had reached the end of my life as it was, and I didn't know how to go on."

He waited another moment, his eyes cast down, his mind apparently giving cautious shape to his thoughts before he spoke them. He looked up. "I questioned everything. I wanted to know why I should go on living. Someone, a friend of mine, gave me a book . . . one of yours, Easwaran. He said, 'Read this.'

"So I read it. After a while, I said to myself, 'Ahhh, so there *is* a purpose in life . . . so *that's* what I have to do.' I started meditating."

He looked into Easwaran's eyes and smiled slightly. "That was four years ago. I've been meditating ever since. I'm able to live again."

His smile widened. "Thanks."

In the classical Indian tradition Easwaran follows, heaven and hell are landscapes of the human mind, metaphors for the turbulent forces that drive us from deep within our unconscious. Meditation helps bring those forces under our conscious control. "Meditation is a sword," he says, "with which we can enter the unconscious and fight it out with the demons that lurk there until we have some say as to what goes on." He adapted his particular method of meditation from such traditional Indian sources as the Bhagavad Gita and the teachings of the sage Patanjali, whose Yoga Sutras define meditation as "controlling the thought-waves of the mind."

It is a demanding discipline. A form of intense, focused concentration, its goal is mastery over the thinking process itself. Easwaran instructs his students to silently recite inspirational passages, such as the Prayer of Saint Francis of Assisi or verses from the Bhagavad Gita, and to bring as much attention to the words of the passage as they can. Sessions grow in length, with careful guidance, from thirty minutes to an hour or more. After much practice ("years," he says, "*decades,*") meditation can deepen a person's conscious attention to such an extent that the thinking process is left behind. All images, all sights and sounds – even, finally, the passage itself – disappear.

What remains? Easwaran quotes Patanjali: "When all thoughts have ceased, you see yourself as you really are."

"In that immense stillness," Easwaran says, "India's ancient sages went beyond the world of space and time. They discovered in the stilled mind a world that was one, a world that was changeless, infinite, radiant with the love of God."

4

As a nurse from Oregon finished her introduction and sat down, silence slipped over the room. The introductions were over. All eyes turned toward the front of the room, where Easwaran sat.

"The people in the back rows might like to exchange

their seats now with the people here in front," he said. There were smiles and laughter from the back rows as musical chairs ensued. But the college-age crowd, heeding a warmly restraining gesture from Easwaran, kept their places on the carpet in front of him. When everyone was settled, Easwaran looked around the room and invited questions. "Practical questions, please."

An alert, serious-looking young man sitting on a pillow in the front raised his hand. He was a freshman at a college in southern California and had started meditating after attending a one-day retreat with Easwaran in the spring. Easwaran's smile was broad now, his tone lightly bantering.

"Yes, Sam?"

"I was wondering how old you were when you started meditating."

"Oh, that was halfway through my life, when I was already functioning as a full-blown egghead."

"Were you really the same as us when you first started meditating?"

A pause. "Not *quite.*" He laughed. "Sam and I have something in common: we are both soccer players. His position is midfield, he tells me. Mine was 'left out.' It is actually an important position in soccer, though I admit the name doesn't sound very respectable.

"For sixteen years, you know, I lived with my grandmother, who was my spiritual teacher, and my mother, whom you might call her teaching assistant – I lost my father early. I had the immense good fortune to be brought up by two remarkable women who apparently wanted nothing more from life than that I be a credit to them. Later, I received an excellent education, combining the best of both the East and the West. So I did grow up with some advantages.

"I was a good, obedient boy in my village. Then, like

you, I went to college and started walking briskly in the opposite direction! When friends used to ask my mother – she lived with us in California for ten years – what kind of child I was, she always told them I was an angel . . . until I went to college. And she was right. I did most of the silly things all young people do. I made some mistakes, mostly at my own expense. But I learned not to make those mistakes again."

He leaned forward. "That's the important thing. I don't expect anyone to go through life without making mistakes. But they need to learn from them early. My heart grieves when I see people making the same mistake over and over again. I wasn't like that at all, and," he said, looking toward the young studcnt, "I'm sure you're not going to be like that either."

Easwaran waited, smiling, as the laughter subsided, then said, "So, I *was* like all of you . . . for the most part."

"Would you comment on how one should go about choosing a teacher?" someone asked from the back.

"My advice has always been to select your teacher with great care. Use common sense, and don't get carried away by personal appearance."

He paused. "You don't go to just any stockbroker and ask him to handle your accounts, do you? You study his record; you ask your friends about him. Now, if choosing a stockbroker can command so much attention, you must pardon me if I say that you should take at least as much care in choosing a spiritual teacher. Look closely at his or her life. That is the surest test. Talk to people who have been with the teacher, who have spent time with him or her. See whether he gets depressed when things go wrong, whether she can return good for ill, love for hatred – whether he can support those who offend him, whether she can forgive those who malign her. How consistent are his actions with his words? I give students years before I accept them fully. I watch them carefully, and I expect them to watch me carefully at the same time. And I ask them to give me a reasonable margin for human error."

An engineer from the South asked, "Sir, what do you mean by the word 'God'?"

"When I talk about God, I am not referring to a being outside us, swinging in a cosmic hammock between the Milky Way and the Andromeda galaxy. I am referring to your deepest Self, to my deepest Self, to that divine spark within which is closer to me than this body, dearer to me than my life. I think it was Saint Augustine who put it perfectly: 'God is inside,' he said. 'We are outside.'"

"What does it *mean* to see God?" the engineer asked with perplexity in his voice.

"To see God means that you see the imperishable Self in every person, regardless of whether you call it the Christ within, or Krishna, or simply the *Atman,* the Self. When I look at Doug and Tom and Kay sitting in front of me, I am aware of their physical appearance, and I even enjoy it. But that is just the outer cover, the house; it is not the resident. The Self is the resident, and it is imperishable; it never changes. So when I look at all of you before me, I see this resident in Sam; in Everett; in you, Richard – the same resident who is one and the same in each of you. That's what God means to me."

Easwaran paused and turned to someone else. Then he looked back at the engineer and, perhaps sensing that he was still perplexed, went on. "When Christine and I were living on the Blue Mountain in India, we were sometimes guests of a European couple who were partial to us. But the husband did not care for the word God. He had some kind of allergy to it. Whenever I would say 'God' or 'Lord,' he would correct me: 'You mean "Nature with a capital N."'"

"Now, I have no difficulty with any of the names people

use to describe God, whether they use He, or She, or even It, as the sages in the Upanishads do. To me, these are all names for the same Reality. So, when we would go to our friends' home and the husband would ask how my mother was getting on, I would reply that she was doing very well, thanks to the grace of Nature with a capital N."

The next question came from a lean man with a dark, clipped beard and quick, intense eyes. A professor of religious studies at a university in California's Central Valley, he had been meditating along Easwaran's lines for several months. "One of the things I like about your book on meditation, Easwaran, is that it doesn't focus on the actual attainment of union with God – I think you call it 'samadhi' in Sanskrit? That is especially gratifying to me because samadhi seems to be so far beyond my reach. On the other hand, I suspect that you have had that experience and that you would want all of us to achieve it eventually. Do you have any comments on that?"

Easwaran drank from his teacup, then set it down. "All that I tell my friends is, give your very best in meditation. Every day. And don't worry about when samadhi comes. When you find a description of samadhi, it may satisfy the intellect. In Sanskrit, *sam*, meaning 'with,' combines with *adhi*, meaning 'Lord,' so the literal, etymological meaning is 'becoming one with the Lord within you.' But words cannot possibly give an accurate description, because samadhi is beyond words. Shankara, whom you know as one of India's greatest mystics, said that samadhi is so ineffable an experience that words turn back from it frightened. The only way I can describe it is through its effect on my daily life."

The professor raised his hand again, and Easwaran nodded. "I can't resist asking one more question, Easwaran, and I think I speak for all of us. I liked Sam's question, were you ever really like us? You seem to imply that you were like us, perhaps up until your thirties, and then something dramatic happened."

"It wasn't really dramatic, you know. It was a gradual process. First I had to play with all the toys of life, as most people do here. The only difference is that in India we didn't get such an ample opportunity to play with life's toys as you people have in the West. So during the first half of my life, my ambitions were not at all spiritual. I wanted to be a writer and a speaker and a good professor. I worked hard at it. Halfway through my life, I had tasted all the success that an Indian could want. Then, everything began to turn to dust. The doors of my consciousness began to open, and a hunger in my heart began to deepen. In time, nothing could satisfy me, not even literature. I began to ask, '*Who am I? Where do I come from? What is the purpose of life?*'

"I began to feel as though someone were following me. There was this voice from within, saying, 'It's time to wake up! It's time to seek God.' And, like a good, educated, cultured young man, I said, 'Voice, get Thee behind me!'"

He laughed. "My initial impulses were very human. I thought that taking to the spiritual life meant the end of my joy and happiness. I wondered, *why me?* There are four hundred million people in this country; what have *I* done? For a long, long time, I thought that all my joy was being taken away, all my goals were being shattered. I tried to drown this voice in literature, in art, in sports and games and movies from Hollywood. The number of Hollywood movies that I tried to drown this in, none of you would believe.

"But it was of no avail. The voice only got louder and louder until finally I couldn't bear it anymore. I had to follow it. And, to my astonishment, I found that it was my grandmother's voice. It was my grandmother's love that had been pursuing me, though I didn't know it at the time. I discovered that she had been my teacher all along and had planted all the seeds of this awakening in my consciousness while I was still a boy – without my knowledge."

He smiled and looked directly at the professor. "And she got away with it, too. I never had a chance!"

Several people raised their hands, and Easwaran nodded toward a woman near the back. "I've read your book on Gandhi and have been very inspired by it. You met Gandhi – I would be curious to know what it was about him that inspired you."

"Yes. You see, when I became troubled by some of these haunting questions, I took them to a lot of wise people who I thought would be able to answer them. I was nonpartisan, so I visited well-known representatives from every religion. They generally gave me a patient hearing, but I am afraid that, to quote Omar Khayyám, I went out by the same door I had come in. They couldn't help me.

"Then I had an inspiration. Why not go and see Gandhi? His ashram was near my campus. I went there and found an enthusiastic band of young people waiting to have his *darshan*. This is a Sanskrit word you may not be acquainted with. It means, literally, 'to look.' In India, we go to an illumined man or woman not so much to converse as to look, to have his or her darshan. Indians believe that when you look at a God-conscious person, it stirs something within you. There is an echo in your deeper consciousness because you are seeing your real Self. Gandhi stirred me deeply by placing before me an image of the human being that was far more radiant than any I had known. He still does. It is this beauty – the same divine spark that is concealed in all of us – that you see when you look at an illumined teacher."

The next questioner was wearing a knee-length brown

sweater and pale tights. An aspiring dancer, eighteen years old, she had heard of Easwaran only a few weeks before and had come to the retreat at the insistence of her college friend John, who was sitting next to her.

"Is it possible to meditate and lead the spiritual life and not to deny your senses altogether?" she asked.

Easwaran smiled, his eyes dancing, and spoke with mock severity. "Becky, where did you get the idea that I ever asked anybody to deny the senses?" He pointed to John, who ducked his head obligingly. "Not from him, I hope!" She grinned and shrugged noncommittally, but waited, listening. She wanted an answer.

"In every book of mine," Easwaran said, "what I ask for is moderation – which is what every good physician will ask for. Moderation in everything. It is what the Buddha called the Middle Path."

He paused. "I'll tell you a story about the Buddha and a young chap just like John here.

"The Buddha was a great artist as well as a superb teacher. He had been trained as a musician, and he was adept in many of the fine arts. One of his disciples was a young fellow who had himself been an aspiring musician until, in a moment of misguided enthusiasm, he gave it up, along with everything else. Word of this got back to the Buddha, and one day he dropped in at the young man's home. After some casual conversation, the Buddha pointed to the fellow's instrument on the wall. 'Well, you have got a vina!'

"'Oh yes, Blessed One, I used to play the vina.'

"'Could I hear something, perhaps?'

"The young man explained that he had stopped playing when he joined the order. 'Why?' asked the Buddha.

"'Because somebody told me that I should deny myself this pleasure.'

"The Buddha asked for the vina. 'May I play it a little?' he asked.

"'Of course,' the young man replied.

"The Buddha quickly loosened all the strings until they hung limply on the instrument. Then he began to play.

"The young man was horrified. Surely his teacher knew better! 'You can't play the vina like that! The strings are too loose.'

"'Of course! You're right,' said the Buddha, and he proceeded to tighten them almost to the breaking point. 'Stop!' the young man interrupted. 'Now they're too tight. They should be neither too loose nor too tight,' he added.

"'Yes,' said the Buddha. 'And it is the same with life. Neither too much nor too little. The middle way.' And, though his biographers don't tell us, I'm sure the Buddha must then have handed the vina back to the young man and asked him please to play for him.

"So you see, I have never asked anybody to deny himself or herself the healthy and innocent pleasures of life. Everything in moderation. That's the message."

More questions followed: on meditation, on work, on trying to meditate within the family context, on love. As they were being asked and answered, dusk had settled. The breeze stopped. An elderly, white-haired gentleman stood up and asked, "Sir, would you please speak on what survives death?"

"That is a question I address in every one of my books. By the time I was sixteen, my teacher had done me a great service by making me aware of my mortality. All people have a superficial fear of death, an intellectual understanding that they will die. But most people don't really *believe* they will die. If they did, they would be making far-reaching changes in their lives, as I did. By the time I left my village for college, I knew death was walking with me.

Chapter One

"It was this deep awareness of the reality of death that finally drove me to meditation, and it was there that I found the answer to the mystery of death. When you go deep in meditation, after many, many years – decades, even – you realize who you really are; you know that you will not die. Like every person, I am aware that my body will someday be resolved into its chemical constituents; but unlike most, I am equally aware that the Self in me will never die. I know, beyond the possibility of a doubt, that I will not die.

"All this came as a gift from my grandmother. As the Gita says, when your teacher has granted you this blessing, what can the world then give you? When you realize this truth, you want to sing in joy to all the world, as the Katha Upanishad says, *Uttistha!* 'Get up!' *Jagrata!* 'Wake up!' and start working toward this realization. You were not made to die. Your body was assembled, and it will be disassembled one day. But your real 'I' will never die. To experience this profound truth in the depths of your own consciousness is the goal of all religion."

A long silence followed in the wake of Easwaran's remarks. All of us had been deeply stirred. The gentleman who had asked the question murmured his thanks, eyes shining. It occurred to me that we could just as easily have been sitting beneath a starry North Indian sky, at the foot of a banyan tree, listening to the Buddha deliver the same message. Nearly half a minute passed before the silence was broken.

"Easwaran . . . " A tall, angular man drew himself up in the back row. He spoke haltingly, his voice resonant with the depth of feeling we had all experienced a moment before. "Easwaran, since I've been studying your teachings, I've become more sensitive to suffering in the world. It's very painful now for me to read a newspaper. When I read about events that go beyond ordinary suffering, it upsets me very much. I wonder if you have any comfort to provide."

"Nobody suffers like the lovers of God, Charles," Easwaran replied, "because they are one with others in *their* suffering. That is the meaning of the crucifixion. But they are granted an equal measure of joy too, because God gives them the capacity to help: to wipe away tears, to make lips smile, to lessen somewhat the burdens of others. When you come to know God in the depths of your consciousness, it means that in a special way you come to know all life in your own consciousness. You have a relationship with everyone and everything in the world. You become aware of the suffering that is at the heart of life, but you feel an accompanying sense of joy in relieving that suffering. Because of this, most deeply spiritual people suffer a great deal, as you are already beginning to discover, but they do not suffer silently, because they know there is something they can do about it.

"Oh, I could easily have said, 'I teach meditation. I don't need to become involved in all these concerns.' And yet, as soon as the tragedy of AIDS began to unfold – right here in San Francisco, the city I have come to love so warmly – I couldn't rest. Millions of people live in the shadow of this terrible threat, and not just those with the virus. I believe that meditation can provide a shield for our beautiful young men and women, all of whom are at increasing risk today and who are very dear to me. The elephant project you heard our children describe, *The New Laurel's Kitchen* – these and many of our other undertakings have sprung directly out of this driving need to alleviate suffering, not only of human beings but of all living creatures.

"It will take a long, long time for these endeavors to be fully realized, and there will be many difficulties in the way. But this is where faith comes in. Gandhi said that there is no selfless prayer that is not answered by God. It's important to add, though, as Gandhi always did, that God answers our prayers on his own terms, not on ours.

"I keep in close touch with what happens in the world. I read a wide assortment of periodicals each week just to do so. And I confess that there are times when I feel deeply grieved by the suffering I read about, and I wonder why life has to be this way. But I never despair. At those times, I go deep, deep in meditation until I reach the very source of love and wisdom that exists in each of us. When I do, I am reassured that all is well. In spite of all the violence and poverty in life, deep, deep down, all is well.

"This is not merely some sentimental notion. I return from this awareness charged with the energy and vision I need to continue to try to alleviate this suffering. So what I would tell you – all of you – is this: meditate every day, throw yourself heart and soul into some form of selfless work, and use your own sense of suffering as a powerful motivation to help relieve the suffering of others. It is a wonderful gift to be able to give."

Easwaran turned toward the audience, then back to Charles. "And remember as you work, Charles, as you struggle with these immensely difficult disciplines, as you face all the suffering and challenges that life will surely bring you – remember that beneath all the suffering and struggle, deep within the heart of every creature on the face of the earth – all is well."

Again there was a long silence. Easwaran looked at his watch. The satsang had gone on for more than two hours. Smiling now, he said, "So, shall we bring these proceedings to a graceful end and have our meditation?"

The lights were dimmed, and Easwaran took a seat next to Christine. Throughout the room, people from the towns and cities of New York and Colorado, Maine and Texas, closed their eyes, drew their backs up straight, and began to meditate. A deep, concentrated stillness fell over the room, joining the silence of the evening outside. If, in that intense silence, an owl called once or twice, or a gust of wind stirred the nearby eucalyptus, many of these people, their attention absorbed in the words of their passage, would not have heard.

Easwaran's ancestral family gathered in the courtyard for a festival, early 1930s

Easwaran's ancestral home

Easwaran's grandmother with her granddaughter Leela, early 1940s. (This photo, taken by Easwaran with a borrowed Brownie, is the only existing portrait of his grandmother.)

Scenes in Easwaran's village in Kerala

Easwaran's mother, about 1976

2 | *Ramagiri*
Teacher and Student

1

Easwaran's day begins early: two hours
of meditation in the gray light of dawn as the quail converse in the willows along the stream bank behind his
room. A short drive to the ocean follows, in all but the
worst weather, and a long, fast walk on the beach with
Christine. After breakfast he looks at the day's mail, then
makes his rounds about the ashram – to the office, print
shop, and bindery; a stop at the school; an apple for the
ashram's chestnut bay horse who grazes nearby. Finally,
a late-morning massage and bath.

Easwaran arrives in the dining hall about one-thirty. As
people eat and chat at one end, he sits in his study at the
other and reads some of the many newspapers and periodicals he subscribes to ("grist for my mill"), or writes, or
talks with friends, or just sits.

From this vantage point, he can see everyone who
comes in for lunch. More significantly, perhaps, they can
see him. Easwaran works within view of his students at
the ashram for long stretches at a time and is available

each day for consultation, spiritual or otherwise. He often jokes that he lives in a glass house. In fact, his study has only a sliding glass door to separate it from the dining room, and even that is usually open.

"This is how my grandmother lived," he has told us. "She was always right in our midst, living with us, working, playing, eating. It is how she was, and it is how I want to be."

In the afternoon, he might go out. An optometrist's appointment could take him to Santa Rosa, where he'll remember someone's birthday and stop at a French bakery to buy a croissant for him. Or he might go to Berkeley or San Francisco, as he regularly does. Watching the crowds on Telegraph Avenue or in Ghirardelli Square is endlessly interesting to him (once again, "grist for my mill"). But more often than not, he stays home and works.

In the past five years, as the sales of Easwaran's books and tapes have doubled, then trebled, so has the work at the ashram itself. Print shop, sound room, and editorial and business offices are all operating in high gear. There are retreats to plan and carry out, and a heavy load of correspondence: people write from all over the world now with questions about meditation or expressions of gratitude. Easwaran reads each letter, sometimes instructing his secretaries how to answer, sometimes answering in his own hand. An organic garden and a whole foods kitchen keep everyone fed, and keep them busy too. Add to all this projects like the RISE program and two wildlife groups, and it's easy to see why such intensity pervades the place – it strikes even the truckers who deliver paper to the print shop.

At dusk, though, the rhythm alters. The presses shut down; the office closes. The evening fog rolls in, and up the long access road comes a string of headlights. The commuters are returning, carpooling as best they can: a reference librarian and two instructors from Santa Rosa Junior College; a physician from a nearby hospital; an architect, an attorney, a printer, a graphic artist, a computer program-mer, and a teacher from Petaluma; a graduate student in statistics from Berkeley; a carload of teenage soccer play-ers and another of after-school swimmers.

Easwaran often talks about the relationship between meditation and the selfless work it is meant to support. We breathe in, and we must breathe out as well. In the eve-ning, as all the activity quiets down, as everyone who was out at work returns, and as one by one we slip into the meditation hall, it is clear: what we've spent so freely we must now replace, from as deep within as our meditation can reach.

Easwaran joins everyone for the evening meditation, and afterward, for dinner. The meal is lively and convivial. Since it is the one time of day when all are together, chil-dren too, a great deal of information is shared: "Several volumes of Easwaran's translation series will be published in England"; "The access road is being resurfaced next week"; "Sixty-five people have enrolled for the November retreat." If one misses dinner, it could take days to catch up. Again, though, it isn't so much what is said; at a deeper level, something is being restored. The food nour-ishes, but so do the warmth, the laughter, and the compan-ionship with which it is taken.

After dinner, Easwaran will occasionally show a video-tape: a movie, selected with the children in mind, or an ath-letic event taped earlier that day – Wimbledon, the Winter Olympics, or a gymnastics meet. Often, though, he will convene a meeting. For people who work away from the ashram, this is the only time of day they can see him.

Late at night, when most have turned in, a light could well be on, still, in the editorial office; the kitchen might be bright, too, as someone weighs out flour for tomorrow's bread. But well after both are extinguished, the reading lamp in Easwaran's room will still be on. He might be reading the memoirs of John Kenneth Galbraith, or something by Jawaharlal Nehru. More likely, though, it's a fairly technical article on the devastation of the rain forests, or a medical journal survey of current treatments for AIDS: material he feels is critical for his work.

It was 9:15 A.M. Easwaran had just returned from his walk on the beach and was seated in the large entry next to the dining hall. The basic pattern of his day is, indeed, predictable, but Easwaran is not one to get caught in unvarying routines. In recent months, he had been stopping by to clean the beach sand off his shoes before returning to his apartment for breakfast. These brief stopovers soon evolved into a kind of forum in which he asked for suggestions about themes for his Tuesday night talks or invited questions on a variety of subjects. Some mornings, he conversed for almost an hour. As this book began to take shape, he encouraged Carol and me to take advantage of these morning visits to ask him about the years of his formation as a spiritual teacher, particularly the village years – his life there with his granny and mother in the extraordinary setting of a matrilineal culture.

Carol sat on one side of Easwaran now, a notepad in her hand. Behind him, through the wide windows of the alcove, spread a landscape of grassy hills and a broad sweep of sky. Stands of willow and alder and an occasional cottonwood followed a small creek down from the hills and past the meadow in front of the hall.

We heard an insistent barking from just outside the door. It was Ganesha, the golden retriever who keeps a close eye on the dining hall and manages to make his presence known whenever Easwaran comes over.

"Will someone please bring a piece of bread?" Easwaran

asked, looking at the dog through the glass. Easwaran carried the crust over to the door, and Ganesha carefully took it from his hand. "This fellow really knows my movements now," he said, sitting down again. "He must have seen us drive in."

Easwaran asked about the children. The older ones were attending a soccer clinic that day, and the oldest girl was taking a driver's training class. The younger children would have swimming lessons that afternoon. Any news from the office? There had been several calls from people who were coming through the area on vacation and wanted to know how to get to the Tuesday night talk, and a good-sized order for our latest book from a distributor.

"And Madeline called to say that she has more than seventy-five people enrolled in her current RISE classes, and at least a hundred are anticipated in the winter," said one of the women from the office.

"Our work is really expanding rapidly," Easwaran said. "So be sure to give your best in your meditation, and stay healthy. If you think there's a lot to do now, just wait. It will get impossible!"

"You don't seem unhappy about it!" Carol said.

He smiled.

"Yes, it's true – I would never have been content living peacefully in some remote Himalayan cave. I would get bored without all these challenges to face every day. That is the depth at which my grandmother lived too."

He looked at Carol and at the notepad in her hand. "Are you ready with questions?"

"I have a lot of them, Easwaran," she said. "But I was wondering if there is anything you want to say before I begin."

"Actually," he said, "there is." He waited for a while before he spoke. Outside, bright sunlight glanced off the leaves of the willows near the creek. "As you know, I had

65

the great fortune of being born into the arms of my teacher, and, in one sense, I have never left them. She still carries me. She was the wisest person I have ever known. All the seeds of what I was to become were planted there in my village, while I was growing up. By the time I left for college at the age of sixteen, all the work had been done by her.

"You see me as I am today, and it may be difficult to grasp how I came to be this way. I want you to understand me and my life, though, not as an isolated occurrence but as the confluence of many streams." He went on to explain what he meant by those streams: the simple, supportive village life itself; the highly devotional, disciplined life his ancestors had led for generations; the examples of some of his teachers and relatives; his parents; and, above all, his intimate relationship with his grandmother. "She probably knew that after I left the village I would have to go my own way for a while, but I was essentially formed. After that, all was a postscript."

He looked at Carol. "Now you start," he said.

"Would you talk about your village, Easwaran? Could you try to describe once again what it was like when you were a boy?"

"First of all, you must realize that much of it has changed since those days, so the life I am describing probably no longer exists. But its beauty, I am glad to say, remains. We were surrounded by lush rice fields, mango orchards, and tall, graceful coconut palms. We got about a hundred inches of rain a year. The heat was tropical, but you didn't really feel it. There were several ponds near our home, and large trees that offered shade and absorbed the heat. The chatter of monkeys and the calls of the men working in the fields were in our ears daily.

"There was no electricity in the village then, and no telephone – no movie theater, no automobiles. In fact, there weren't even bicycles until the day my father pedaled into our village on one and rode it around the compound of our ancestral home. We couldn't believe it. It seemed supernatural, a conjurer's trick."

Basic needs were met locally, Easwaran explained, and from local materials. Homes were built of bricks made at a kiln right in the town, and of teak from the adjacent forest. "The foundations go deep," he said, "so that despite the dampness of the climate, the houses can last hundreds of years."

Their diet was simple and wholesome. Rice, home-grown and unprocessed, was the staple. Bananas, mangoes, and jackfruit grew abundantly, and so did a wide variety of vegetables and pulses. "My grandmother loved greens, and almost every day we ate them in one form or another. We had our own cows, too. She tended them herself."

From its genesis, the village had been virtually self-sufficient. Many centuries ago, his ancestors had lived much farther to the south, and when they came north they brought carpenters with them to build their houses. The carpenters were given land to build homes for their own families, as were potters, a blacksmith, weavers, a barber, an oilman, a priest, a garland maker for the temple, and a goldsmith. The positions were hereditary, so the lineage of the local potter or weaver may have extended about as far back as the Eknaths' own.

"Everything was close, and we always felt interconnected. The potter's house was just a block away from mine, and I would go down there and watch him, fascinated. The weaver would come by and say to the potter, 'I'll make you a new wearing cloth if you can turn out a water pot for my wife!' They would dicker and laugh together. It was wonderful for a child to be able to see all this – real work, and skilled.

"The goldsmith used to come around to our house

regularly, and the girls would gather in a knot around him on the veranda. He would get out his little portable stove, fuel it with straw, and set up the crucible. Then my girl cousins would show him just what they wanted: a pendant shaped like a mango leaf, or earrings that hung like open umbrellas. Right there on the veranda he would melt down the gold and form the jewelry according to their designs, as they watched."

Easwaran's village was remote from any urban center (in fact, Kerala state has no big cities), but culturally it was very much alive. South India is renowned for its classical music and dance, and for Kathakali, an ancient and highly developed form of dance-drama. Traveling Kathakali troupes would come through several times a year and stay in the Eknath family compound for a week at a time.

Performed at night, in the flickering light of coconut-oil lamps five or six feet high, Kathakali was a riveting spectacle – at once rich entertainment and inspiring religious instruction. Drums would call villagers from miles around. Wearing elaborate and very stylized costumes, the dancers would use a richly articulated language of gestures and movements to act out stories from the Hindu epics, their performances often lasting until dawn. Easwaran would sit throughout the night, snug against his grandmother's side, until the last demon was exorcised, the last noble lovers reunited.

Seven miles from his village, moreover, was the town of Palghat. In South Indian classical music circles, Palghat is a name to conjure with. "Palghat is known all over India for the exacting standards it imposes on the would-be professional musician," he told us. "If you can make it in Palghat, you can write your ticket anywhere in India." Easwaran's father was an ardent patron of musicians, and one of Easwaran's uncles – his favorite, Uncle Appa – was a classically trained musician.

"It was a rich, simple, intimate, secure life, which formed us with deep bonds of familial love. Everything we needed was right there in the home. My elementary school was on our own veranda. After school we would play soccer in a fallow peanut field, then plunge into the cool river nearby for a swim. We had enough cousins to make our own soccer team. I had close friendships with dozens of cousins, girls as well as boys. Growing up, I took it all for granted. It was only later that I learned the inestimable value of such a life.

"And it was in the midst of all this that my grandmother spent her entire life. She worked hard. She took part in all the festivals; she shared all our joys and sorrows. Yet, to my knowledge, the awareness of God never left her, not for a moment."

Easwaran talks and writes about his grandmother frequently. Yet you always feel that something about her is eluding you – that there is something vital you haven't quite taken in. Carol may have felt that way now, for after Easwaran stopped for a moment to take a drink of ice water, she asked him, "How do you think your grandmother came to *be* that way?"

"You have always to remember, Carol, that I come from a matrilineal society, which sets it apart from every other society I know of. The stream of our consciousness flows through the women, and that alters our whole pattern of relationships."

"Was there a stronger sense of equality between men and women in your family than, say, in other parts of India, or in the West, for that matter?"

"It was more than equality," he said. "To us boys growing up in that large family, the women were looked upon as superiors, young as well as old. You see, the high values of our ancient civilization have been transmitted mainly through our women. Even as boys we sensed that they had received something of its wisdom that we had not." He laughed. "They knew something we didn't know . . . and they knew it!

"The women in my family had an enormous inward assurance. Even as a boy, I used to go to some of the girls for guidance. It seemed the natural thing to do. And they helped me, too. This is simply part of my family's ancient tradition. What you see in me, whatever it is that you find appealing, is really the product of the contribution of hundreds of these women down the ages. I have simply become the fruit of the tree which they nourished."

"And the women sensed this?"

"Oh, yes!" He recalled an incident from more than twenty years before. "When Christine and I visited my village before coming back to this country, one of my aunts told me, 'When you go back there, don't forget to tell them that we women taught you all this.' It was true. And my grandmother, of course, represented the finest fruit of that tradition."

"You've said that she never had a teacher?"

"My grandmother, as far as I can make out, was always full of God's awareness. She must have been born that way. She didn't talk about her spiritual awareness, and she had only one student – me – though I didn't know it at the time. To me she was just Granny. She functioned so freely and naturally among us that it took me decades to realize that she was an extraordinary human being."

From as early as he could remember, he said, his grandmother had been devoted to him, and he to her. "We were inseparable. I was known throughout the village as 'Granny's boy.' It caused me some embarrassment, especially when I got older, but I cherished the name. There was nothing I would not have done for my grandmother."

He looked again at Carol and her yellow pad. She was ready with another question.

"This may sound awfully . . . journalistic, Easwaran, but if you had to use just one word to characterize her personality, in contrast to all the other good, kind people that you lived among, is there a word you would use?"

"Yes," he said without pause. "She was free."

"In what way?"

"In everything she did. See, my grandmother had no constraints, and no compulsions either. At mealtimes, she ate with a vigorous appetite. She really liked to eat. But she didn't think about it. Once she had finished a meal, she forgot about food until the next one." Her sleeping patterns followed a natural rhythm as well. "When nightfall came, she would unroll her grass mat, lie down, and fall asleep within a few seconds, as naturally as a child. She didn't even use a pillow. She said it put a crick in her neck."

And she could be fiercely independent. "She didn't want to have to depend on anyone. She learned to milk the cows herself, talking to them, calling them by name, treating them when they got ill. She did a lot of the work around the house even though there were servants to whom she could have entrusted most of what she did. And when my aunts asked her why she did all these things – some were not 'appropriate' for a woman of her station – she just quietly told them, 'Your own gums are better than someone else's teeth.'"

He laughed. "She was quite an original."

His grandmother loved physical activity of all kinds. She was a good swimmer, and she loved to dance. When the younger women danced for religious festivals, she always joined in. "No one would dance more vigorously – or more gracefully. People would stop what they were doing and watch. She would joke, calling down the line, 'I think someone might have two left feet!'

"She didn't like her movements to be hampered, so she would wear her sari tucked up high – she had beautiful feet and ankles – and there used to be a running exchange between her and the younger women of my family, who wore their saris more fashionably long. My grandmother would tease them: 'Oh, good, now I won't have to sweep the floor!'"

She had a native sagacity about life that sometimes ignored the dictates of custom. For example, rice was normally cooked in a large quantity of water, which was then discarded. "In other families it was given to the cows, but my grandmother saved it and we drank it. It became a kind of joke in the village: only Granny, her boy, and the cows will drink that stuff, people said. And as it turns out, modern nutritionists would have applauded her."

"What did she look like to you?" Carol asked. "How do you remember her?"

He smiled, recalling. "Oh, slim and golden brown. She had the figure of a teenager, and she walked like one too: graceful, quick, lithe." But, like many mystics, she hardly identified herself with her body. "When she had a rare bout of illness, she would say, 'Oh, I am quite well. It's this body that is giving me some trouble.' I would ask her sometimes how old she was – her parents had both died when she was quite young, and there were really no records – and she would look at me, baffled, and say, 'How would I know? Why do *you* want to know? What does it matter?' It was as if I'd asked how old was her wearing cloth, or her sandals."

He paused. "She had found her security within herself, you know, and nothing could shake it."

Similarly, his grandmother was never intimidated by religious and caste distinctions. "In our tradition, one of the hallmarks of the God-conscious man or woman is *sama-drishti*. It means seeing equally – seeing the same Lord in everyone. My grandmother was like that. Religious or class or caste distinctions did not restrict her. She never preached about this, though. It's just the way she was.

"She didn't distinguish much between old and young, either. The notion of a generation gap would have been unthinkable to her. Unlike most of the elders in my family, my grandmother would play games with us children. She used to play doubles with me in marbles, and together we often beat my cousins. Her concentration was so keen she could give any of them a handicap and still win. And she played hard!"

He stopped a moment, remembering something. "There was a small tree by the south end of our veranda that bore a very delicate fruit – like your Bing cherry, only more . . . bing! Once the fruits were ripe, my grandmother would gather all the children below, climb up into the tree, and shake the branches. The fruits would rain down while we did our best to catch them.

"She had a real affection for all the younger people in our family, but she was especially attentive to the girls." For the great feasts, about a hundred people would come to his ancestral home. His grandmother would sit up most of the night with the younger women, helping them chop vegetables and keeping their spirits up. "I think now that that was her way of training them to work together in harmony. When a young girl was new to cooking, there were always some mistakes, and some of my aunts would get a little starchy. But my grandmother would always encourage them. 'If you don't burn a little and spill a little,' she maintained, 'you'll never learn to cook.' They all loved her for it."

Carol smiled noticeably at this point, and later I asked her why. She explained that it had been a long time since she had heard Easwaran use the "spilling and burning" story, and it was a favorite of hers. During the early years with Easwaran, when we and several other Berkeley students were first struggling to put his teachings into practice, he had invoked it often. She and her housemates would get discouraged because they had snapped at one another or backslid in some other way, and he would console them with his grandmother's advice to budding cooks. But she reminded me that he had always added, "*Learn* from your mistakes. If you go on burning and spilling, you'll never learn how to cook!"

Now she said to him, "Easwaran, you said that your grandmother was free of religious distinctions as well. South India is especially orthodox in its religious customs, isn't it? And your family was an ancient one which had built its own temples. How orthodox was she?"

"Well, you could say that my grandmother was orthodox in a very unorthodox way. She was so full of devotion, and so deeply aware of the Lord within her, that I don't think she needed external observations. Yet she did observe all the rituals and customs of our village society. She didn't follow them for the sake of social convention, though. She enjoyed them thoroughly."

As an example of her "unorthodox" orthodoxy, he explained that she felt quite comfortable going to any one of the several different temples in the village – not a common practice among devout Hindus, who generally worship a particular *ishta*, or chosen deity. "In our ancestral village, the temple at which most of my family worshiped was the Shiva temple, yet my grandmother worshiped just as freely in the Krishna temple or the temple of the Divine Mother. She was at home in any of these traditions because she knew, on the strength of her own experience, that all of them led to the same goal. And I absorbed this, you know: the truth is the same by whatever name it is called. That was how she planted those seeds in me."

"Do you think she had some idea that your own spiritual development wouldn't be along orthodox lines?"

"Yes. In fact, she encouraged me to rebel. I never responded much to ritual, and she knew that. She would ask me to come to the temple with her perhaps once a week, or on special occasions. I would always go when she asked. And in her presence, by a kind of osmosis, I would feel deeply devotional. But I knew even then that it was her presence, and my love for her, not the temple or the ceremonies, that brought this about.

"You see, my grandmother was not trammeled by any conditioning. She could be deeply orthodox, yet she could break away easily. She just was not bound by custom, and this was made apparent to me very early on."

He paused awhile. "Oh yes!" he said, a look of surprise on his face. He had remembered something. "Now, to give you an example of how freely she could act. When a solar eclipse takes place, orthodox Hindus fast. My grandmother observed this tradition to the letter – for herself. But where I was concerned, she saw no reason to be bound by the custom. After all, I was a growing child; I was going to school, I needed my breakfast. But rather than upset the household by openly defying the custom, she would send me off to the home of a friend whose mother saw things Granny's way. I would take my books along early morning, eat breakfast there with my friend, and study until it was time to go to school.

"Of course, we didn't say anything to our family about it. It's a matter of honor, you know, that you don't give your granny away."

He grew serious. "You see, caste, gender, age, religious outlook – none of these bound her to the conditioned preconceptions of her society. She functioned perfectly within a social framework that was often quite narrow, yet at the same time she transcended it. I absorbed all this, and it proved endlessly valuable when I came to the West."

He looked at Carol. "Do you see what a breathtaking accomplishment this was? All the time, while we were living in a situation that was completely defined by restrictions of one kind or another, she was preparing me to slip easily into a setting which had no restrictions at all."

He looked off toward the hills. "There was just nobody like my grandmother."

"But she had some help, didn't she?" asked Carol.

"Yes. My grandmother was my spiritual teacher; I have no doubt about that. But she could not have done her work without the support and influence of my mother."

Only one photograph is placed in the ashram's meditation hall. It is of Easwaran's grandmother. In the photo, which Easwaran himself took using a Brownie camera borrowed from a college friend, she stands erect in a white cotton sari beside her young granddaughter. Behind them is the wall of the ancestral compound, draped with the branches of a pearl jasmine tree Easwaran had planted as a boy. (His grandmother picked its leaves to use in her daily worship.) She is looking directly into the camera, and brilliant sunlight throws a shadow over one side of her face. Her look is firm, almost severe in the intense light, and the figure is one of unmistakable strength.

Similarly, there is only one photograph in the ashram's dining room, and it is of someone who looks very *like* Easwaran's grandmother. It is his mother, who lived at the ashram for the last ten years of her life and who passed away the same winter that the dining hall was built. In the photograph, which hangs beside the dining room's wide brick hearth, she is holding a small brass lamp. The whole impression is one of glowing, incandescent warmth and light. And indeed, she was all tenderness and accessibility. Residents of the ashram remember her sitting over tea each morning in the kitchen of the cottage she shared with Easwaran and six others when we first moved to Ramagiri – a tiny, fragile figure clothed all in white, gazing with keen interest out the kitchen window, keeping a close eye on everyone's comings and goings, particularly the children's.

Easwaran's grandmother, on the other hand, was austere, from what he has told us – overpowering, even, to many who knew her. Despite her domestic setting, her real realm was otherworldly – the spirit, and its struggle for freedom.

Carol asked about his relationship with his mother. How did it compare with that with his grandmother?

"Though different," he said, "it was as close. She devoted herself completely to me, and at some level I knew that. Her influence on me was profound. She had immense purity – the quality Jesus was describing when he said, 'Blessed are the pure in heart, for they shall see God.' In all the time I knew her, I never heard her speak an unkind word about anyone. I suppose that explains why I just can't bring myself to speak harshly about anyone, no matter what the circumstances."

"In what ways was she different from her mother?"

"My grandmother was taciturn and could be solemn. My mother was always sociable, even gregarious – and naturally so. She was easily approachable, and she loved to talk. I don't think she ever met a person she didn't like. My grandmother could be very severe with me, but my mother was just the opposite. They were very close, and the only time I can remember them having any differences was over me. My grandmother always took, you might say, the 'hard line.' Never my mother.

"You see, they were devoted to each other. They went

to the temple together every day; they ate together, slept near each other. Until my grandmother shed her body, in her seventies, hardly a day passed when they didn't spend some time together.

"And together they made me what I am."

He paused and looked at me. "What time do you have?" It was ten o'clock.

"I had better go. Christine is waiting."

"I'm right here." The Virginia-accented voice came from the stairway opposite the alcove, where Christine was seated, smiling broadly. Easwaran was surprised – she had come in so quietly that no one knew she was there. He took her hand and, talking and laughing together, they walked over to their apartment.

2 | The world Easwaran inhabited as a small boy was a world of charm and loveliness – in many ways idyllic. Yet even as he was growing up, the idyll was vanishing. The great landholdings were breaking up, and the young people were starting to go to the cities to find work. Eventually, some would go to other countries as well. Then too, technology was reaching even this remote village, and it would transform life in a thousand small and definitive ways.

"It was very much the world that Chekhov describes in *The Cherry Orchard*," Easwaran said. "The older people looking back, feeling bewildered, even embittered, some of them, not ready for the world they found themselves living in."

It was another sunlit morning in the alcove, and Easwaran was describing the slow erosion of his privileged family life. While the others of her generation were looking back, he explained, his grandmother had been looking ahead. She could not have known how rapidly it would all change – how dramatically different his life would be from hers. And yet, uncannily, she was preparing him for it all the time.

Carol had asked him if he would talk about the daily round of his early life with his mother and grandmother.

He was always an intense boy, he recalled, with powerful passions and a deep affinity for animals. "If there was something I loved, I had to make it mine." When a stray dog wandered into the family compound, he adopted it, the first of many dogs he would raise and love, and the very first, for that matter, to enter the family circle. He reared a pigeon that roosted, when it could, on his shoulder. Painfully sensitive to the suffering of animals, he could not resist trying to do something about their suffering, even when he knew his help would be of little use. He remembered long nights during the monsoon season when he couldn't sleep because of the plaintive croaking of frogs being caught by snakes. He would go out into the night and move the frogs where he hoped they would be safe. His grandmother knew better, but she encouraged him anyway: "Even if it doesn't help the frogs," she said, "it helps you."

Sometimes, listening to Easwaran describe his years with his grandmother, it seems that it is not just a set of memories he is recalling. It is, rather, like a book, a kind of scripture that he is still reading and still coming to understand. Episodes that had only charmed or amused him before begin to reveal deeper meanings, and as he relates them he communicates a certain awe at his grandmother's stature.

He gave that impression this morning, as he again seemed to be moving toward a clearer understanding of the significance of his time with his grandmother.

Carol asked him how his day would begin.

He recalled mornings as a child, getting ready for school

while his mother and grandmother prepared breakfast. "I woke up each morning to the music of my grandmother singing her mantram as she swept the veranda. We slept there together, my grandmother and I. She always liked the fresh outdoor air, and so do I.

"My mother would start the cooking, and if the cowherd, Appu, was late, my grandmother would go out and start milking the cows. Now, at other homes the children had to wait for their milk if he was late. But not me. My grandmother would go out and milk the cows herself, and I would help her. I would have to hold the calf while Granny milked. It is not an easy thing to do. The calf is trying to nurse, and the mother wants to lick the calf. So you have to hold it back. That was my job. See, that was one way she taught me not to depend on other people."

The milk would be boiled and breakfast eaten in the kitchen, the boy sitting on a grass mat on the floor while his mother and grandmother brought him hot rice cakes and dosas right off the stove. Even at this early hour, all three would be chattering away.

"Would it be just the three of you?"

"Ordinarily, yes." He smiled then, remembering. "Except on the mornings when Appu came."

"Would you say more about Appu? Didn't your grandmother have a special relationship with him?"

"Yes. She never allowed social conventions to stand in the way of her choice of friends. Appu was the village cowherd, and he was a remarkable character. He took care of fifty or more cows. Each morning he would come around to all the houses and take the cows out to the meadows to graze. Each cow was named after one of our goddesses, and he could call them by their Sanskrit names: 'Kaveri, come here – your rope is tangled in your horns!' And she'd come! For each one he got a rupee per month. He used to tell the headmaster of our elementary school, 'I make more salary than you do, and I have better students, too!'

"Appu adored my grandmother, and she was very fond of him, which was highly unusual within the restricted conventions of village society. And somehow he used to manage to turn up at our house regularly, just when breakfast was being served. 'Oh, well, I couldn't possibly,' he would say. You know, the polite protests people make. But he would happily eat the steamed rice cakes and coconut chutney that my grandmother would serve him. I used to get annoyed, because I wanted her full attention. Finally I said one day (I was only six or seven), 'Appu, why do you always come at this time? You must be coming just for our rice cakes.' And you know, his answer floored me. 'I can get rice cakes at any home,' he said. 'I come here so that I can receive them from your granny's hand.' I was ashamed.

"My grandmother trusted him completely. When there was a fair or festival I wanted to attend, she didn't send me with an uncle. She would entrust me to Appu's care with complete confidence. This was true even though she knew he was rather fond of toddy, a potent alcoholic beverage brewed from coconut milk. She knew he wouldn't drink when he was with me, no matter how he was tempted. He would call me *Yajman*, which is like 'Milord.'"

"Wasn't Appu a boxer, too?" I asked.

Easwaran smiled and told the story of how the deceptively gentle Appu had defeated a local bully in a boxing match while his small charge watched in terror from the sidelines. Life in the village, we were to understand, was not just the family veranda. It was rich, earthy, and plainspoken, as was his grandmother.

"Easwaran, doesn't your family name actually carry a title?"

"Oh, yes, but I stopped using it very early on – when

I came under the influence of this country, in fact."

"Why did you decide to drop it?"

He smiled. "I decided that I wanted to stand on my own two feet and not rest on the glory of my ancestors."

Easwaran is an educator, first and last – supremely at home in a classroom. Though his search for meaning took him far beyond the academic setting, he retains great affection for that world, and he sets a high value on intellectual training. Just how deep the roots of those feelings go becomes apparent when he speaks of his own education.

"School began at ten o'clock," he told us, "and to get there on time, I had to start on the footpath by nine-thirty." His grandmother marked a certain point on the veranda. When the shadow of the roof reached that point, she would instruct him, "Start running!" "And I did run," he said, "not because I was afraid of being late but because I was so eager for school to start.

"But my grandmother had no sense of time, really." He shook his head and laughed. "That's one of the problems of spiritual awareness. It takes you out of time! Once, when I was in high school, I had to study for a physics test. I asked my grandmother to wake me at four. She woke me up, and I got right down to my book. I went through light, electricity, magnetism, sound – the whole book. And still the sun wasn't up. She had wakened me at midnight!"

Easwaran's initiation into the world of letters was celebrated with deliberate ritual by his family. A few months before his fifth birthday, he found himself seated on the veranda with his family gathered around and the temple priest next to him. Sand had been carried up from the river and spread out carefully before them. The priest fitted a hollow berry onto Easwaran's fingertip, took the boy's hand in his own, and, leaning forward, guided the small hand as he traced in the sand, with large and sweeping strokes, the first letter of the Malayalam alphabet.

"My grandmother stood by, smiling proudly. 'See,' she said, 'he is taking the curves well!' She herself was illiterate. But she understood that this would have much significance for my future."

His first schoolteacher was a spiritual seeker who had wandered all over India and who wore the saffron robes of a renunciant. And his first schoolroom was the veranda itself. "Our family believed that having a hereditary teacher is as important as having a hereditary carpenter, so we supported him, gave him a house and a part of the veranda as a small classroom. This same man had taught my mother too – just the three R's, but she was quite proud of her reading prowess. In fact, I recall that once when my mother and grandmother had a rare disagreement, my mother teased Granny by reminding her that she could read and write, while Granny could not. 'And you don't know how to swim!' Granny retorted.

"What my first teacher taught me was the supreme importance of training the memory. 'Cultivate your memory every day,' he would tell us, 'and it will be prodigious.' He had us learn the multiplication tables up to sixteen-times – forward and backward – in Malayalam. I can still do it."

Not long after he began his schooling on the veranda, an elementary school was built in his village, and the schoolmaster asked his grandmother to send him. A few years later, a secondary school opened. "It came in a grade at a time," he said, "staying just a year ahead of me all the way."

Some of the young men in the village, who had until then been unable to continue their studies, came to the new secondary school. "It was hard for them because they'd been out of school so long. They were like older brothers. They kept an eye out for us and didn't ask for anything in return. Except during exam time, when they would lean forward and whisper, 'Write larger, please!'"

"Was the high school coeducational?"

"Oh, yes. My girl cousins attended it, including one who was much older." He chuckled. "At the end of the school day, she would hand over her books to us. 'Carry these home!' she would tell us, and walk off! That's the thing about these matrilineal cultures; you can't just say, 'Excuse me, I was going to go play soccer!'"

"When did you start learning English?"

"I had picked it up a little bit at a time, starting with the letters of the alphabet when I was just six or seven. Probably by the time I was ten, I could read it. But the wonderful thing about the high school was that English was the medium of instruction. Now I could really make progress. Three of my uncles were on the staff, all fine scholars. One of them taught Malayalam, another Sanskrit; and another, Uncle Appa, was my English teacher. He was also our 'class master,' which is like your home room teacher. He was over six feet tall and quite handsome. He was a gifted classical singer and could have been a successful artist, but he chose to stay in the village and share his love of music and literature with us.

"And soccer. Uncle Appa was an amazing soccer player. He probably could have played professionally. I adored him. It was he who first encouraged my writing."

"Was he the one who first got you interested in English literature?"

"Yes, that was Uncle Appa. He introduced me to Palgrave's *Golden Treasury*, the standard anthology of poetry in all British schools. I memorized many of the poems in it, including the whole of Gray's 'Elegy Written in a Country Church-Yard.'" (Easwaran's talks are still

sprinkled with lines from Byron and Wordsworth, Gray
and Milton – lines that he committed to memory as a boy.]

"Did your grandmother encourage you to learn English?"

"Oh yes. In fact, she thought it was a marvelous feat.
She would ask me to say something in English, and just to
amuse her I would point to the well and say 'water.' She
would shake her head in wonder. She wouldn't say 'Speak
English,' though, but 'Speak ABCD.'

"Carol, this will give you an idea of how wonderful the
atmosphere was that I grew up in. I came home one day
from playing soccer – I was in high school at the time – and
my grandmother pulled me aside and pointed to one of the
rooms in my ancestral home. The doors were closed, and I
could hear voices inside. She said, 'Go on in there, Little
Lamp. You'll enjoy it. They're speaking ABCD!' I opened
the door and saw my Uncle Shankara – he was a lawyer
who practiced in Madras – and several friends. They were
practicing the assassination scene from *Julius Caesar*. Imagine!"

Easwaran's scholastic promise became more and more evi-
dent, and the family elders decided that when he went on
to college he should study engineering, a highly paid profession and one that would surely put him in great
demand.

But they hadn't reckoned on the headmaster of his
high school, an exacting man who ran the school along
decidedly British lines. "His great passion in life was gram-
mar. He was always especially strict with me, as he was
with one or two other students. He used to say, in front of
the whole class, 'This boy, he will never use a shorter
word if he can find a longer one,' and he said it at every opportunity! It was true, I confess, but it stung, and it took

me a long time to understand that he was hard only on those in whom he saw promise."

One day the headmaster called him into his office and took a book from the small collection he kept locked in the cabinet behind his desk. This was the school library. The book was Sir Walter Scott's *The Talisman*. "Read this," he said. Easwaran took the book home and read by the light of his hurricane lantern. Much of the night he read, and the next night as well, lured by the spell of Scott's medieval enchantment. A door opened, and a new world beckoned. He returned the book and asked for another. He read Trollope, Thackeray, Eliot, Dickens, Austen. In a short time he had finished the collection locked behind the headmaster's desk and started over.

"It was like waking up on a new planet," Easwaran told us. "I couldn't believe what I was reading. It was not life as I had known it, but a world of wonder. I moved from poetry and novels to dramas and short stories – I just couldn't get enough." His enchantment began a decades-long romance with English literature.

"I would keep a hurricane lantern on the veranda to read by. 'Don't you think it's time you got to sleep, Little Lamp?' my grandmother would ask. I would say, 'Just one more chapter, Granny! I have to find out what's going to happen to Sam Weller.' She would remind me twice. Then she would just reach out and turn off the lantern.

"She never let me get away with *anything*. There was one occasion when one of my more worldly cousins came to me – taking pity on my innocence, I think – and said, 'You know, there's going to be a performance in the next village tonight. Don't tell your granny, but I think you'll like it.' Now, these were pretty racy programs – like the American vaudeville, only very down-to-earth humor. I'd heard enough about them for my curiosity to be burning high. The show was late at night, so by the time my cousin came my family was asleep. He had what I thought was a highly sophisticated idea of putting pillows in my bedding so it would look as if I were there asleep. We tiptoed out and went to the show. It was pretty bad. Afterward, I came silently back onto the veranda and slid between my blankets, pleased that I hadn't disturbed my granny at all. Then the silence of the night was broken with just one word from her. '*Nishachara,*' she said, and went back to sleep. I was mortified. That's a Sanskrit word, you see. *Nisha* is 'night'; *chara* is 'one who creeps around' – it's the name of a demon! You can be sure I never did that again!"

He laughed with us, but then leaned forward slightly. "The point is, she could have just stopped me when I was first slipping away – she was well aware of what I was doing. But she wanted me to find out for myself."

He returned to his theme. "I adored books. The world of Victorian England became more real to me than my village. You who have grown up with this world of literature cannot fully understand what it meant to someone like me, growing up in a small village far from the cultural centers of the West. To me, it was a living world."

He paused and took a drink of ice water. Through the window behind him, a pair of deer had edged from the willows near the creek and onto the grass outside the alcove. Easwaran hadn't seen them. He went on. "But my education was not only from books. My grandmother knew the value of books, but she had a native sagacity that showed itself in what she insisted I learn outside of school."

"Like learning how to swim?"

"Yes, that was one. There were two skills that she especially insisted I acquire. The first was swimming. This wasn't just for safety, but because she was so bent on erudition . . . mine.

"You see, when I was in elementary school, the closest

87

high school was in a village a few miles away, and a river ran between that village and my own – not just a creek, but a good-sized river. During the monsoon season the river would sometimes be swollen, and you'd have to swim across it or be truant. As you know, a high school opened in my village just in time. But meanwhile, my grandmother had taught me to swim, right there in the pond at our home."

"And the second skill?" Carol asked.

"Riding an elephant. Why she was so intent on this nobody understood at the time. But she saw to it that I learned to ride one, and at a much younger age than children normally learned it, if they did at all. I couldn't have been more than seven. She loved elephants dearly, but that was only part of the reason."

"How did you learn?"

"The hard way," he said. "No cushion, no straps to hold on to. An elephant is a four-seater. It can hold four children, and no more. Usually my cousin Shankari would sit at the very front, with a soft seat and ropes to hold. Very safe, very comfortable. Behind her would be a younger boy, then another, still younger. By now, when it came to me, things would be getting wobbly. At just the point where the elephant starts to slope dramatically, that was my seat." He laughed. "This was hard enough to maintain when the elephant was standing still, but when he started to move it was all I could do to stay on. I kept hauling myself up and clutching at the boy in front, who didn't like it one bit. I didn't blame him!

"Finally, though, I did learn – and I rode an elephant at all the festivals."

"What do you think your grandmother's deeper reason might have been?"

"In India, whenever we see an elephant, we are reminded of the immense power of the Lord. In fact, in our spiritual tradition the elephant symbolizes the Lord's power to remove obstacles – great ones or small ones. And it is our belief that when you love the Lord, some of that immense power comes to you – power to remove the obstacles in your own path, and in the paths of others as well.

"Of course, before you can love an elephant, you have to get over your fear of him. It is a very natural fear, after all, for these are huge creatures. My grandmother wanted to be sure I overcame that fear, and for her I did.

"What I want you to realize about my grandmother is this: there *was* danger in my doing this at such an early age. That didn't bother her in the least. Hers was a very rare kind of love."

He smiled. "There was another thing she wanted of me, curiously enough, and that was that I should become a Boy Scout. Here her motives weren't so deep – I think she just wanted to see me in the green turban that Indian Boy Scouts wore. I learned how to send Morse code, and my cousin and I would send messages between our two houses, just tapping with sticks. Tap tap . . . tap tap tap . . . and so on. And my grandmother would be dumb with amazement. She would give me a word, I would send it to my cousin, and he would run over and tell her what she had said. She just couldn't get over it."

Carol said that she found the image of all those large-eyed Eknath boys in khaki shorts and bandanas oddly touching. "It is so . . . British," she said. Easwaran smiled.

"Yes. In fact, soon after I had my tenderfoot badge I was asked to lead our troop in presenting the honor guard when the British governor was visiting Palghat. We were very impressed with the occasion – felt very inadequate to it – and that was just how we were meant to feel. All that pomp, you know, was very cleverly designed to intimidate us. I had never seen British people before, and the soldiers were all wearing helmets with long points on top. It was astonishing. And the ladies all wore tall, very high heels. I couldn't stop staring – we could only assume that the men fought with their heads!"

We all laughed, and someone mused, "And that the ladies fought with their heels?" He grinned but maintained a gallant silence.

"Was the British presence felt much in your village?" I asked.

"Not really. They stayed mainly in the big cities," he said, "and on the cool mountaintops."

He remembered that from the veranda where he and his grandmother slept, they could see the summit of the Nilgiris, the Blue Mountains, where British colonials and their families escaped the sweltering summers. There were picturesque English villages, golf courses, tea shops, and cottages with names like "Fern Dell" and "The Glades": a transplanted English countryside in miniature. Standing high above the subtropical plain, the Nilgiris seemed remote and almost magical to the young boy.

"One of our neighbors had a summer home on the Blue Mountains, and he would talk about the evening fogs there, the tea plantations, the English. These touched my imagination. The mountains looked like another universe to me." During the monsoon season, lightning would sometimes ignite fires in the bamboo groves on the mountains. "From where we slept on the veranda we could see the fires. My grandmother and I would lie there, watching them glow against the sky." The fires would form what looked like a necklace, he said – a string of flame across the dark throat of the hills. It was to the Nilgiris that, decades later, he would move his mother after the passing away of his grandmother, and there the world of tea plantations, evening mists, and incisive British humor would become his own.

As Easwaran spoke to us in the alcove, the two deer had

been moving across the meadow and now stood browsing near the window. There had been no deer when we moved here in 1970. The land had been overgrazed and left with little food or cover for wild creatures, and the stream itself was badly eroded. In the succeeding years, as we planted trees and erosion-resistant shrubs and grasses, the stream banks were gradually transformed into a small forest. A herd of deer now lives in the dense undergrowth, and their presence gives Easwaran great satisfaction.

"See how close they come now," he said in a soft voice.

3 | It is probably safe to say that no concept is more central to the Indian mystical tradition than that of the spiritual teacher. It would be difficult to imagine Indian spirituality without it. And it is perhaps equally safe to say that in the West there is no concept in Indian mysticism that has caused more misunderstanding and distortion.

Several days had passed since Carol had asked Easwaran about his relationship with his grandmother, and today she wanted to ask him about Granny's role as his spiritual teacher. First, though, she wondered if he would talk in general about the subject itself. How did he define the role of the teacher? What did it mean to him?

"The idea of the spiritual teacher is actually quite simple," he said. "Just as you need a guide to scale a mountain peak for the first time – someone who has gone before – you need an experienced guide on the spiritual path. You need someone who can show you the way, help you when you get tied up in your ropes."

The experienced teacher, he explained, is one who has made the climb to the top, then returned to the lowlands. Not out of a personal longing, but out of a great urge to share – to find the handful of students who are prepared, and eager, to face the rigors of the climb. "The teacher should know every inch of the ascent, from the foothills to the summit. He should be able to warn his students where there are ice fields and crevasses, where they can pitch their tents and rest."

"And the role of the student?"

The student, Easwaran said, must take all the steps himself, including the supremely important one of choosing a teacher to begin with. He wanted it understood, "beyond a shadow of doubt," that the teacher does not make the journey for the student. A spiritual teacher is just a signpost pointing out the direction.

"Actually, it is more accurate to think of the true teacher as your innermost Self, the Atman. The role of the outer teacher is to help the student become aware of the teacher within. To the extent that a person is loyal to the outer teacher, to that extent he or she is being loyal to the deepest Self."

"You know, Easwaran," Carol said, "it seems that typically when people gravitate toward you – when they start coming to Tuesday night talks and begin to meditate – it isn't always because they're conscious of wanting to establish a relationship with a teacher. For Americans, the whole notion of asking someone to be your spiritual teacher is, well, problematic. Taking up meditation, that's not so overwhelming. What is it that usually moves an individual to seek a teacher consciously, actively?"

"Many things," he told her. It was his experience, he said, that people become interested in meditation for various reasons. Some hope to solve long-standing physical problems which may have resisted other modes of treatment. Others come to him because they want to solve emotional difficulties which prevent them from forming lasting relationships. "I don't mind acting as a last resort for such persons," he added with a smile. "In fact, some young people have come to me just to get through finals. That's all right, if they find that it helps. But they still have to study." Still others want to unlock creative resources they feel to be "blocked" inside. "All these are limited, short-term ends," he said. "But there is another group, young and not so young, who have played with the toys of life and found them to be . . . just toys. They have weighed life in the balance and found it wanting."

Such individuals are not looking for a stopgap solution, a temporary cure to a momentary dissatisfaction. "They want to know, is there no purpose in life? Why are they in this world? What is the meaning of death? These are the men and women I most value guiding in meditation, because they want to go all the way. They want to get to the root of their dissatisfaction, to the source of suffering itself."

"Do people ever move to that second group once they've solved the problem that brought them to you in the first place?"

"Regularly," he said, smiling. "A great many of the people who are meditating with me now did just that. The desire for Self-realization is at the core of consciousness in every human being, and often all the teacher has to do is, in the Buddha's words, blow the dust from their eyes. When their vision clears, that desire will flare up."

I asked him what he most looks for in people who want to become his students. "Enthusiasm," he said without hesitation. "I tell them, 'Don't worry about your past mistakes; don't stay away because of guilt. Just begin. Start meditating, then see what changes can be made.'"

"Would you explain what qualities are required for a person to be a spiritual teacher?" Carol asked.

"Only a genuine and repeated experience of the Self. The lamp must be lit within. When a person becomes aware of the Self, of God within, he or she is not strictly a

person any longer, but a spiritual force. Gandhi was a
force. Saint Teresa was a force. In this sense, they both still
live and are active. It matters not at all what talent or crea-
tivity or charisma a person may have; if the lamp is not lit
within, charisma means nothing. If you try to become a
spiritual teacher without becoming established in this
inner experience, you will take yourself and your students
to disaster."

He paused a moment, then continued. "I get alarmed
when I see some people in the West acting as spiritual
teachers without access to the deeper resources that come
with Self-realization. I don't think they are fully aware of
the awesome responsibilities on their shoulders, which
can become unbearable. I never knew anyone in India who
tried to become a spiritual teacher. There is a lot of grief in
the life of a teacher, a lot of anguish. You feel everyone's
pain as your own. People there know how formidable the
responsibility is. A spiritual teacher has to have the capacity to bear a lot of suffering. And you have to be on duty all
the twenty-four hours. It's not a job you apply for – it finds
you.

"The student has a primary responsibility in looking
for a teacher, and that is to resolve one question: does the
teacher live for others, or does he live for himself? This is
the true test. For the lamp cannot be lit until all self-will
has died out."

There can be no doubt, Easwaran has said, that his grandmother knew he would follow in her spiritual footsteps.
Unlettered, taciturn by nature, she did not express this in-
tuition except to tell him more than once that he was not
like other boys. "I used to protest when she told me that,"
Easwaran said during one morning's conversation. "I
would say, 'I *am* like other boys, Granny. I may be bright,
but there are a lot of bright boys.' She wouldn't argue with

me. She would just end the conversation: 'You are not like other boys.'"

Every day during vacation, his cousins would go out to play soccer while he went to study Sanskrit. "In the heat of the midday sun, I hobbled to the home of the temple priest on traditional wooden sandals in order to learn this 'language of the gods.' I asked, 'Why me, Granny? Why not the others too?' But all I received was the same remark: 'You are not like the others.'"

Nor was she like other grandmothers. Revered in the village for her strength of character, she had a passionate devotion to God and regarded Him on an intimate, even familiar, basis. Her day circled around a Presence as real to her as eating and sleeping, and each day was rounded, morning and evening, with worship at the family temple. She talked to Him, and was even known to scold the God who refused to send rain during a long dry spell. She had a will "of steel," and when she set her mind on a thing, no villager, no family member, old or young, relished standing in her way. Nor, apparently, even the great God himself.

"The priest at the Shiva temple used to tell us, 'When Granny calls to the Lord, the Lord answers: "Yes, Big Mother?"'"

Carol asked if he would talk about how his grandmother actually gave him spiritual instruction.

"She never formally instructed me, Carol. That was not her way. She didn't know how to express these truths in words. She taught by example, by her love. And I just absorbed her lessons – almost by osmosis, you might say."

Would he give an example?

He thought for a few seconds and smiled. "My granny could be very original. You see, she didn't like to have the people around her quarreling. It pained her very much. And it happened once that two of the branches of our extended family became embroiled in a bitter quarrel. So it posed a dilemma when, on some special occasion – probably a festival – both sides of the family expected my grandmother to come for the main meal. Whichever place she went, the other side of the family would feel insulted. My grandmother thought the whole business was plain silly. My mother suggested she tell both branches that she would rather stay home and be with her immediate family. That was the easy way out, but Granny never liked an easy way out.

"She looked at me and said, 'Little Lamp, are you equal to two lunches?' I said I'd try. So she accepted both invitations, much to the consternation of my mother. On the appointed day, we went to the first place and had a fine lunch. In fact, I got carried away with the jackfruit pudding and started to eat more of it than I should have. It was a favorite of mine, and it was good! She signaled to me to stop halfway. She didn't say anything, just a few eye signals. It was a great conflict for me, because I wasn't sure they would have it at the other place. But I managed to stop. It was like braking a car going sixty miles per hour. As we left, my grandmother looked at all the women there (it was the women who were quarreling) and said, 'We have enjoyed your meal very much. Now we are going to go to the other home and enjoy their meal very much too.' We went there – and gave a good account of ourselves, too!

"She never failed to set an example, even to the elders in the family, when they were acting foolishly – especially when it was the women. She had a flair for bringing people together.

"But I can give you another, even more vivid, example of how she taught me. This was the time that my cousins and I came home late from our soccer game, running along the banks between the paddy fields. At twilight the paths could be crawling with poisonous snakes who had come out to take their evening walks. In the fading light they were hard to see and therefore were doubly dangerous. You could step on one before you knew it was there." His grandmother had told him more than once to leave for home before twilight set in, but, lost in the game, he just couldn't manage it. Then one evening he found her waiting for him on the path. "She was standing, barefoot, next to a snake-infested bush. She didn't say a word. She didn't have to." He didn't come home late again.

"That was the kind of love she had for me, and that was how she showed it. Of all the ways of giving spiritual instruction, the highest and most effective is through the living, personal example of an illumined teacher. That is why it is said in our tradition that spiritual awareness is not so much taught as caught.

"See, the way she went about teaching me was all so natural that I wasn't even aware of it. I just saw her as my grandmother. And yet, at a much deeper, unconscious level, I must have had some idea of her significance to me."

Would he explain what he meant?

"It's difficult to explain," he said.

He spoke slowly. "When I was still a boy, perhaps twelve or so, my grandmother contracted cholera. She became gravely ill, and the doctors despaired of her life. I wasn't told this, and though I knew she was quite ill, I had no idea she might die." His mother spent every moment tending her as she lay on a small cot in a room removed from the main family quarters. "Cholera usually takes three days to run its course," he said. "One day the doctor told me I should go see my grandmother. He didn't say why. I assume now he expected me to say good-bye.

"When I entered the room, I saw her lying quite still on the cot. My mother was next to her. My grandmother's eyes were closed, and there was no movement: even her

face was still. She must have been very near the end.
I watched her lying there, and I saw the look on my
mother's face. For the first time I understood how grave
her condition was. The thought of losing her filled me
with an anguish I could not bear. I broke down. They
tried to get me to leave. I just stood there and cried out,
'Granny, don't leave me! If you go, what will become of
me?' They tried again to get me to leave, but I cried out,
over and over, from the depths of my being: 'What will
become of me if you go?'"

Finally, he was led back to his room. Later his mother
told him that not long after he had been taken away, she
had felt a tremor pass through his grandmother's body.
"Shortly afterward, she opened her eyes. She looked
around without moving and saw my mother. In a voice
that was barely audible, she whispered, 'I'll take some tea.'
My grandmother loved her tea. Within a few hours, she
was sitting up and talking quietly. She lived another
twenty-five years."

Easwaran waited again before speaking. "It wasn't just
her and it wasn't just me, Carol. It was the love between
us that became the medium through which she taught.

"All that time, all those sixteen years, my grandmother
was teaching me, though I didn't know it. She was laying
the groundwork for the time when I would be forced by life
to undertake the journey of Self-discovery. By the time I
was sixteen, my grandmother had done her work. She probably knew I would have to go my own way, and suffer
some blows."

It was his grandmother, in fact, who insisted he leave the
village and go away to college. "She knew that this step
would take me to a way of life that would keep me from
her, but she also knew that it was necessary if I was going
to learn to stand on my own."

He did not want to leave the village. "She almost forced

me to leave her," he said, "though it cost her greatly. I found out only later just how much it did cost her. But I didn't understand any of this at the time – only much later. If I had understood it then, I would not have gone so far away. I probably would have denied myself the kind of education this work would require. She must have known this somehow.

"I heard much later that in those years after I left the village, my mother and grandmother would go to the places where we had been and would talk and reminisce about our time together. I probably should have taken both of them with me, but at sixteen I just didn't have the maturity to understand all of this.

"'Follow your own star,' she told me more than once. 'Go and learn, and share all that we have given you.' She knew she had done her work, and she wanted me to be independent. She even trained my mother not to hold on to me so that I could learn to carry out the mission she believed I was destined for. So she sent me away. Greater love than this you will not find in this world."

He looked at Carol. "So you mustn't think of my grandmother as the doting type who sat in a rocker on a porch, knitting and smiling, giving me everything I wanted. She knew her purpose in life, and she knew what she had to do to achieve it. As I have said many times, she could be tough. She did not suffer fools gladly. If she thought I deserved it, she wasn't afraid to use corporal punishment. And I don't remember her ever saying, 'This hurts me more than it does you.' Yet I never doubted for an instant that she loved me more than she loved herself.

"Once, I remember, I began a casual remark to her by saying, 'Granny, when I die . . . ' But she slapped my face before I could get the rest of the words out. I was stunned. Tears welled up. 'Granny! Why did you do that?' She looked as fierce as I can ever remember her looking. She took me by the shoulders and said, 'Little Lamp, you will never die. I don't want to hear you talk such rubbish again!' How could I understand that she was teaching me the most important lesson in life?

"My grandmother's life was a mirror of the divine splendor of the Lord, the love and wisdom that lie within us. It was all I needed. That is why our tradition maintains that even if all the scriptures were lost, we could reconstruct them from the life of just one illumined man or woman. It would be sufficient."

The meditation hall at the ashram is a former chapel built by Catholic monks who once lived in the Victorian farmhouse next to it. Its walls are bare except for two large brass temple lamps that stand in niches at the front. The photograph of Easwaran's grandmother is mounted on a stand below.

Each evening, after meditation, Easwaran pauses in front of this picture. He stands unmoving for ten or fifteen seconds, sometimes longer.

One morning Carol asked him what he was thinking about when he stood like that.

His look drew inward. "I say to her, 'Where would I be without you? *What* would I be without you?'"

Seated second from the right with his college classmates, about 1930

Late 1930s

In graduate school

At his first teaching position (seated, second row, second from the left), with members of the faculty and the student debating society

At the beach, 1969

With niece Geetha, 1970

At a picnic, 1969

3 | Sand Point
Years of Growth

1

At about eight-thirty each morning,
weather permitting, Christine and Easwaran drive their
burgundy-colored station wagon through several miles
of small hills cropped close by grazing sheep, then down
the rim of a coastal ravine to the parking lot of a narrow
beach. Exercise is an unvarying part of Easwaran's routine,
and for the past fifteen years he and Christine have regularly walked along this shore.

On a recent spring morning – brisk, with a slight breeze –
Easwaran invited us to join them. Arriving early, we took
seats at a picnic table near the sand-covered parking lot
that separates the road from the beach. The morning air
was cool, a sharp, crystalline lens that made the ridge to
the south loom closer than it was.

After a few minutes, Christine and Easwaran arrived
and alighted from the station wagon. Easwaran pulled on
his gloves and dropped the flaps of his hat over his ears.
Christine took his hand, and we all struggled across the
soft sand to the firm surface along the edge of the surf that

is best for walking. Easwaran stopped for a moment and looked out at the ocean. The view of the Pacific was un-broken, a flat, blue-gray sea knitted with flecks of white at the horizon – the fishing fleet from a nearby harbor. The north end of the beach is bounded by sheer sandstone cliffs, rubbed raw by wind and high seas: a dramatic view, but too short a walk. We headed south.

The two of them set out at a brisk stride, and we fell into step behind them. Two gulls rode the air currents above our heads, calling loudly, while a cormorant sailed down the crown of a long wave, then turned back toward the cliffs. A long wall of dunes was just rising on our left when we caught sight of a round shape listing in the foam at the water's edge. We slowed down. Tipped upward by the surf was the decaying body of a California sea lion, rocking softly in the swell. Easwaran stopped a moment, looking at the body, while the surf heaved the creature another foot up the beach.

Gently, Christine touched his arm, and we were off again. A hundred yards farther on, we hopped a stream of runoff water and regained our stride near some timbers half-buried in the sand. We moved quickly down the beach, the breeze coming toward us from the southwest, only the sky and the sea and the ample dunes framing our view . . .

Carol and I were glad of the chance to come along this morning. When he walks here, Easwaran often stops for a while at the south end of the beach, and we hoped we might be able to ask him there about the circumstances that had finally led him to take up meditation. Over the years, he had told us about that period of his life in bits and pieces, but never in a sustained way. "I was sixteen," he had told us earlier that week, "when I left my village to attend a small Catholic college. It was only fifty miles

away, but you must understand that in that part of the
world, in those days, distances were much longer. I confess
to you that I had mixed feelings about leaving my grandmother and my mother. I loved them so much that the
thought of being cut off from them was almost unbearable.
But my grandmother insisted I go away to college. I missed
her terribly." Every chance he found, he took the train
home to see her. His friends couldn't understand: his
grandmother!

"Once I didn't have money for a ticket, but I went down
to the train station anyway and asked the railway guard for
a ride. 'Hey,' he shouted to the other trainmen, 'This boy
wants to see his granny!' He let me ride with him in the
guard's compartment all the way."

He has hinted at what a difficult time that was for him,
that first year away from his village. But he has a certain
reluctance to dwell on it, so it is from Christine that we
have been able to understand more deeply what he was up
against.

"From all I've gathered," she told us, "he was quite
disoriented at first. He missed his grandmother and his
mother so much that it was hard for him to apply himself
to his studies. He never *could* bring himself to study for
grades, anyway, and he was still trying to go along with
the family's idea of his becoming an engineer. So there he
was, taking mathematics, physics, and chemistry but actually spending most of his time in the library, where he'd
discovered a complete set of Dickens."

Over time, things straightened out. Father John, the
principal of the college, was a consummate scholar and
an astute judge of students. He was quick to see the boy's
enormous potential and take him under his wing. Under
his tutelage, Easwaran began to speak and debate – and did
so impressively. His mentor was not easy on him, though.

"He would sit in front at all the debates," Easwaran recalled, "and one day after a competition he called me into his office. I thought I'd done rather well. He took his time. 'Did you eat your breakfast this morning?' he asked. 'Yes, Father, I did.' 'Did you get enough to eat?' 'Oh, yes, Father, I ate plenty.' Then he leaned forward and asked with fierce emphasis, 'Well, then, why did you swallow the words at the end of every sentence?' I was really taken aback, but you know, I never forgot! He didn't go in for praise; he was very much like my granny in that."

Easwaran had just begun to feel comfortable as a speaker when one day the college messenger came to his class.

"'Father John wants to see you immediately!' he said. I went to his room with my feet trembling in my sandals.

"'I want you to represent the college in the intercollegiate debate at Alwaye,' he said.

"I was astonished – and alarmed! I didn't say anything about my not being Catholic; I just stammered, 'But Father John, I'm not equal to it. I'm sure to break down on the platform before such a large crowd! What if I lose? . . . as I am sure to!'

"He shrugged and, with a nonchalance that terrified me, said, 'Then don't come back.'

"Full of misgivings, I went to the debate. It was held at a beautiful campus situated by the river in which the great Kerala mystic Shankara had bathed more than a thousand years ago. I was fortunate enough to win the trophy for our college, and I celebrated by swimming in the river with my fellow competitors. I was enormously relieved. When I met Father John on the following day, though, all he said was, 'Oh – I see you came back.'"

Time and again, Father John demonstrated his affection and support, but never overtly. There was the occasion, for example, when Easwaran's grandmother hadn't been able to send the fee for his examinations. Easwaran was distraught: no fee, no exam; that was the rule. A list of students who had paid was posted in the main hall, and though he knew it was hopeless, he nevertheless found himself searching the list. There, to his amazement, was his name. Someone had made a mistake, he decided. It would be found out. It would be best to go straight to Father John.

"Come in," came the deep voice from behind the door.

"Father, my grandmother couldn't send the fee for the examination. I cannot take the exams."

In his stay at the University of Edinburgh, Father John had acquired fluency in three languages, a comprehensive knowledge of English literature, and the habit of smoking large cigars. He was smoking one now. "Well?"

"But . . . there's been a mistake. My name is on the list!"

"It is on the list, you say?"

"Yes, Father."

"Then somebody must have paid your fees!"

Silence, and sudden comprehension. Smoke curling toward the ceiling. "Now go on and let me finish my cigar in peace!"

"He taught only one class," Easwaran recalled. "That was Shakespeare. I sat right in the front, my eyes riveted, not missing a word. He spoke with a slight stammer, and even now I remember with affection the way he would say 'Sh-Sh-Shakespeare.'

"I kept his picture in my room. Even now, sometimes, I have dreams about his coming here and my showing him around our ashram. I think he would be pleased."

Easwaran's college years marked his first sustained contact with Christianity. (His village had been populated only by Hindus and a handful of Muslims.) "Father John was a true Christian. He taught me more about Christianity than all the books I have read. I even attended his church on occasion, and it set rumors afloat in my village that I had 'gone over.'

"Everyone in my family got alarmed when they heard this. Except my grandmother. She knew it was out of my respect for Father John that I went there."

Over the next couple of years, Easwaran's passion for literature deepened immeasurably. Torn between that love and his sense of duty, Easwaran went to his grandmother and unburdened himself. "She only told me to follow my own star," he said. "So, finally, I did. When my elders discovered that my courses at college were loaded heavily on the side of literature and languages, they tried to persuade my grandmother to apply pressure, knowing I would do anything she wanted. It was on this occasion that she told them all, 'My boy is going to be the king's messenger.' They were as puzzled by this as I was," he went on, "but she gave me the freedom to grow in my own way, even when it went counter to the ancient customs that regulated her own life. In fact, she actually encouraged me to rebel against orthodoxy, seeing into me far more deeply than I could see into myself."

A receding tide had left small piles of debris that lined the edge of the surf and occasionally slowed us up. We stepped over and around them – mostly heaps of driftwood and kelp. Phalaropes moved in and around the debris, pecking at invisible meals.

We moved in silence, and at a good pace. No one spoke, since this was a perfect time for silent repetition of one's mantram. If twenty years' habitual practice hadn't prompted us, the steady sound of the sea itself would have done so.

The benefits of meditation itself may not always be felt right away, but the calming, invigorating effect of walking while repeating the mantram can be experienced easily –

and all the more powerfully in company. Easwaran recommends it often as an antidote to emotional stress. As soon as you find yourself feeling angry, afraid, or insecure, he urges, go out for a fast walk repeating the mantram. The mind will be racing at first, and breaths will come fast and shallow. But the rhythm of your footsteps will blend with the rhythm of the mantram, and in time your breathing will slow to the same deep and calming rhythm.

With typical catholicity, Easwaran suggests several different mantrams from all the world's religious traditions for his students to choose from. Many choose a mantram from the tradition they were raised in, while many adopt Easwaran's. The mantram is a powerful tool, he says, to drive the awareness of God into the deepest regions of consciousness. Each repetition brings you closer to the abiding source of security within.

On our left, a gap in the dunes revealed a high hill of sand sloped gently along one side, with a more precipitous face on the other – a popular beginner's jump for hang gliders in the area. It was still early as we passed, and the bluff was empty, its trackless surface polished by the night breezes.

Just offshore, another sea lion bobbed – this one very much alive, even playful. The alert, whiskered little face would pop up, then disappear under the water in an impromptu game of hide-and-seek. Someone remarked how doglike the sea lion looked, and Easwaran told us that in Malayalam the word for sea lion does in fact mean "sea dog." We walked on toward the mouth of the narrow bay at the end of the beach.

What distinguished Easwaran in his academic career, he has told us, and later in his teaching, was not just his aptitude ("There were always better scholars than I was") but his passion for the written word. "I simply couldn't get enough of it," he recalled. "My whole world was in books, in literature, poetry, drama. The world of literature was a paradise for me. It was all I wanted." One night some friends asked him to help them understand the main themes in the development of English literature. "It was a full moon night. We had tea brought in, and then I began. I lost all track of the hours that were passing. By the time I was finishing with the Romantic poets, the sun had come up. It was the next day – and the fellows were still listening!"

Shakespeare, Milton, and the Victorians were special favorites, but his interests were not confined to the literature of England. Greek and Roman history fascinated him, and he read extensively in that area. Continuing his studies in Sanskrit, he read widely in classical Indian literature and took a particular interest in the ninth-century dramatist Kalidasa, whose poetry and profundity compare favorably with Shakespeare's. Easwaran's competence in both Western and Sanskrit literature was rare even in India, and it helped him to bridge Eastern and Western cultures. "I owe all that to my uneducated grandmother, and to her insisting that I learn Sanskrit."

By his own account, Easwaran was a passionate individual. His initials, he jokes, stand for "Extreme Enthusiasm." Each stage of his life has been marked by strong attachments – to family, to friends, to literature, to animals, to the many students who have studied literature with him or come to him for spiritual guidance – and, not least, his all-consuming devotion to his "Beloved Boss," Sri Krishna, who, he says, has installed himself in Easwaran's heart. Indeed, it is Easwaran's deeply passionate nature that has helped to shape him into the kind of teacher he is today: intensely personal and untiringly dedicated to his students. And it was also the force that, as he puts it, hurled him "out of the village and into the soup."

He was intensely curious about life, and once he got over his initial disorientation, he lost no time in finding out about it. "I looked around and saw that there were people on my campus who were having a good time – and they were not doing what their grandmothers wanted them to do. This had never occurred to me!" It was not long before the deferential, cautious "granny's boy" from the village began to experiment. "I was like a little frog from the well, suddenly let loose in a big pond.

"I probably became a little brainwashed, for example, by the movies I went to with my friends. Indian films were relatively restrained – nothing like the Hollywood films that were shown in larger towns. Still, even in those days, they didn't always offer the highest models. My friends would forget about them afterward, but if something in them attracted me, it wasn't enough for me just to watch. I had to act on it. Not only that, in my college library there were copies of British humor magazines, like *Punch* and *For Men Only*. By modern standards they would seem quite innocuous, but for a young boy just out of his village, they were pretty inflammatory. I began to believe, and act, as though the sensory world were the only real world. I didn't do anybody any harm, except myself, but I was no longer the selfless 'granny's boy' I had been in my village."

In the tightly connected world of a Kerala village, news traveled quickly. "Sometimes the reports of my behavior managed to reach my village before I did. But my grandmother always stood by me. She understood that I would have to experiment with life. It speaks infinitely of her that she never said I was not worthy of her. Once, when I came home after one of my questionable episodes, she said to me, 'You are such a bright boy. How can you do such foolish things?' That stung."

Education in British India during Easwaran's student days was generally sound and in some ways exceptional.

But never was it intended to inspire a sense of worth or dignity in its colonial clientele. The Indian history that Easwaran learned was steeped, he explained, in the cultural biases of the Britishers who wrote and taught it, and their Western attitudes (and inaccuracies) were passed on to the Indian students themselves. It was not surprising, he said, that he began to regard Western culture as innately superior to his own. Most educated Indians shared his belief. In Easwaran's case, enamored of the world of Dickens and Thackeray, he fell happily under England's spell: "I really came to believe that the answer to most of our problems lay with the West. I owe a great debt to England and the cultural legacy I received from her. But it led me to commit a lot of mistakes, too. I didn't have the discrimination in those days to see either the weaknesses in Western culture or the great nobility and strength of India's spiritual tradition."

The "mistakes" Easwaran laments comprised what would be considered a natural course of development in any professional setting, East or West. He pursued personal goals and satisfactions, and he was ambitious and successful. There was nothing reprehensible in any of this, but set against the selfless, spiritually charged example of his grandmother's life, his own development, he believes, fell far short.

"She watched all this happening, and to her credit she did not interfere with the direction she saw me taking. She simply told me more than once that it was not in life's capacity to make a selfish person happy. She didn't mean it in a moralistic sense, only as a quiet observation. And she was right, of course, but I couldn't understand it at the time. At that point, I was far more concerned with my place in history than with the meaning of life." His grandmother stood aside, waiting for Easwaran's own self-knowledge to correct his course. "She knew that I would outgrow all of this, and she knew that the seeds she planted in me would eventually bear fruit.

"How she knew this I can't say. But I am awfully glad I developed the way I did. It cost me a lot of pain, but I'm a better teacher for it. My personal acquaintance with the satisfactions of the senses, personal success, and the delights of art and the intellect, *and their limitations:* all this made it possible for me to be a creditable spiritual teacher in the West. Now, if I had lived a monastic life in some cave, why would you people who grew up in L.A. and Brooklyn have listened to me? As it was, I underwent the same influences, the same painful trial and error that most of you have gone through. Without this experience, I would have been a far less effective spiritual teacher. And, in some unspoken way, my uneducated, village-bound grandmother understood all this."

At the same time, she could be ruthless at his expense. One weekend he returned from college in shoes, knee-high socks, khaki shorts, and a blazer. When his grandmother saw him coming, she called out to his mother, "Ammalu, come look at this brown English boy!" Another time, many years later, he returned to the family compound sporting what the British called a "topee," the round sun helmet that was the emblem of British imperialism. (He had picked it up secondhand, liked the look of it, and had given no thought to any symbolic import it might have.) His grandmother said nothing. The next morning, however, the helmet was nowhere to be found, until he wandered outside looking for his grandmother. There it was, inverted in her hands: a fine basket, she explained, which she was filling with flowers plucked for temple worship.

By the time he graduated, Easwaran had become a prominent campus figure, at home in the world of scholarship – and in front of an audience. Before going on to graduate school, while spending some time in Secunderabad, in central India, he had the opportunity to observe many world-famous speakers at the local YMCA, which he visited frequently with some of his Hindu and Muslim friends. He joined the Toastmasters club there, and, making good use of the public speaking skills first encouraged by Father John, he soon became quite a draw.

For his graduate work, Easwaran went to the University of Nagpur in central India to receive higher degrees in English literature and law. India's system of higher education was modeled after that of Great Britain: within each subject area, all university graduates underwent the same examinations. The scores would then be published simultaneously in selected newspapers throughout the country, with a student's score listed next to his or her identification number.

When Easwaran was taking his examination, he became so absorbed in answering a question on the Elizabethan period (his specialty) that he failed to allow himself enough time for the remaining questions. "I hurried the rest of my answers and went home dead certain that I had missed my opportunity."

On the given day he went to the local newspaper office and searched the second-class listings for his number. "I didn't find it," he recounted. "I wasn't even listed in the third-class section. I had done even worse than I feared." But then the editor suggested he check the first-class listings. "You never know," he told him. Easwaran shrugged.

"But by that time I was desperate," Easwaran told us, "so I looked at the first-class section." He checked the numbers on his ticket, then looked again at the list. There were his numbers, listed under both English and law.

First-class degrees in English and law should have been sufficient, but these were still the days of British rule, and

not at all the best of times for a young Indian academic.
"Most of the best teaching jobs went to Englishmen,"
Easwaran said, "especially in my field, English literature.
They ran the university system, and they made the place-
ments." He had to wait. A few years passed and he seemed
to be getting nowhere; life was passing him by. He com-
plained more than once to his grandmother that despite
his qualifications and his demonstrated abilities, he could
not get a teaching job.

"She just told me, for the thousandth time, 'That is not
what you are meant to do. You are not like the others. You
are going to be the king's messenger.' I didn't know what
to make of it."

Finally Easwaran received a position at a small college
in central India.

"I came alone, knowing no one and having no idea
where I would live. I signed the papers to take up my
charge, and when I came out of the president's office,
there, to my complete surprise, was a beloved friend
from graduate school. Naimuddin, a Muslim, was a
gifted scholar of Persian and Urdu. I had lost track of
him completely, but he had seen that I was to be posted at
his campus and was there waiting for me with his horse-
drawn tonga. My luggage was in the back. 'Get in!' he said.
He took me to a splendid Moghul mansion built in the
eighteenth century – with swords and sabers hung on the
walls – where he was staying while the owner was on
pilgrimage in Mecca. I stayed on there for a couple of years
even after the nawab returned. Naimuddin was transferred
to another post, but my host, a most gracious Muslim aris-
tocrat, continued to treat me as an honored guest."

Easwaran was very much at home on the beautiful
campus and felt that he was exactly where he wanted to
be. "Those years just before India achieved her independence were very electric times, you must remember. The

atmosphere was seething with the desire for India's freedom. In many ways, being on a campus then was like
being in Berkeley during the late sixties."

At last he was able to share his passion for Shakespeare
and Shaw with students as eager to learn as he was to
teach. Morning and evening he would pedal his bicycle
to and from the campus – he was known as the slowest
cyclist in town – and always there would be students riding alongside.

"Through Naimuddin, meanwhile, I was being drawn
into a delightful world. He loved the glories of Persian
poetry and helped me come to love them too. There were
evenings when with his friends we would take turns reciting *The Rubáiyát of Omar Khayyám* in English and Persian, and students would come in great crowds to listen.
This was academic life at its richest; to my knowledge, I
couldn't have been happier."

During the years that followed, Easwaran established
a national reputation as a columnist for *The Times of
India* and a story writer for the *Illustrated Weekly of
India*. Valued as a regular speaker on All India Radio, he
was in growing demand as a lecturer. Then he applied for,
and won, the position of full professor and chairman of the
English department at the University of Nagpur, where he
had attended graduate school. His growing fame had not
hurt his chances, nor had his popularity with the students.
"I loved my subject so much," he said, "and I loved to
teach. I sometimes wondered why anyone would pay me
to do it."

His prospects could hardly have been brighter. "I was
finding as much success as any Indian could have hoped
for," he told us. "I could not imagine a happier way to
spend my life." All things being equal, it is likely that he
would have done just that: lived out his charmed life as

writer and academic, "lost in the world of books and plays and poetry."

All things, apparently, were not equal. He was not like the other boys, his grandmother had insisted. He was going to be "the king's messenger," she had said. And she, as he would come to understand more fully with the passing years, was certainly not like other grandmothers.

2

When we stopped walking, the neck of the slender bay that runs inland from Sand Point lay before us.

Easwaran stood on a small spit and looked out at the ocean. A high ridge formed the shore on the other side, cutting our view to the south. On a landing close by perched three brown pelicans, oblivious to our arrival, beaks bowed solemnly to their breasts. Easwaran walked over to a large log, brushed a spot free of sand, took off his gloves, and sat down with Christine. Carol and I sat down on the sand.

For a moment we just sat, savoring the sense of well-being that comes of vigorous movement and the quiet pleasure of Easwaran's company.

He was the first to speak.

"This terrible disease that is killing our sea lions. What is it?"

"It's a kind of lung infection," I told him. "No one is quite sure what its origins are. It's communicable to some other mammals. I know, for example, that dogs are supposed to be kept away from any sea lions that might have the disease."

"Is it related to pollution?"

"I don't think anyone knows, but it's definitely on the increase. There used to be outbreaks every ten years or so, but the last one was only four years ago. Some authorities

think water pollution may have something to do with it –
maybe because it interferes with the animals' immune sys-
tems."

Easwaran looked out at the waves, visibly troubled.

I asked him if he would mind telling us what he had
been thinking when he was looking at the dead sea lion
we had seen earlier.

"When I see the body of an animal who has died, it's
much more than the death of a single creature that sweeps
over me. It is as if the curtain of a great tragedy rises, and
the stage of life and death is opened. It is partly my own
death I feel, partly that of everyone: all life hurtling toward
its end."

I asked if he would explain.

"You see, when you are continuously aware that all life
is one, your awareness reaches out into the world like an
open nerve. It registers both the pain and the joy of its creatures. It is the price to be paid for becoming aware of the
underlying unity of life."

We were silent for a moment, then Carol asked, a little
hesitantly, if he would talk about the effects meditation
has on him now. "I mean," she added, "obviously, meditation for you now must be very different from what it is for
us, and even from what it was for you twenty years ago.
Your mind is already effectively stilled, so what are you
doing when you meditate?"

He smiled, then answered emphatically, "I can only say
that there is nothing like meditation. Even now – after
what, almost forty years? – it is still so fresh. As you know,
I sit for meditation more than two hours every morning,
and again at night. And each morning, in the depths of
meditation, I see a clear, changeless reality that continu-
ally refreshes my spirit and quickens everything in my life.
As a result, I never get bored. I never take life for granted.

"The vision of the underlying unity of life makes every

moment come alive. You forget about the past. You stop fretting over the future. See, I have no expectations from life, and I have no regrets. Without expectations, I no longer live in the future. Without regrets, I don't live in the past. I am all here, and because of this, every moment is alive." He explained that the sense of living completely in the moment is characteristic of the mystical life. It enables the mystic to see the miracles of life every day, in every moment. He quoted Blake, who, looking at the sun, saw not simply a round spot "the size of a guinea" but "a heavenly host crying, *Holy, Holy, Holy!*"

"What more can I say? That is the vision that comes in the climax of meditation. With an inner wisdom you see that nothing is insignificant, that ultimately, everything fits. Every person, every creature – we all have a place."

There was silence for a moment. I was trying to absorb the immensity of what he'd just said.

Across the bay, small clouds had appeared and were drifting inland. Only a few people were visible on the beach, and one small sailboat struggled against the surf at the mouth of the bay. "*We all have a place . . .* " Yet not two centuries ago, the shores of this very bay had been dotted with the villages of indigenous Coastal Miwok Indians: Echa-Kolum and Shotomko-wi, farther up the bay; Sakloki, not far from where we sat on Sand Point. According to local historians, the Miwoks were a peaceable people who lived here for millennia in huts made of willow and tule, eating acorns gathered from the woods and shellfish scooped from the bay at low tide. Under pressure from the Spanish, the Miwok societies collapsed by the mid-nineteenth century, and the Indians were reduced to servitude. As the Indian culture went, so went the abundant wildlife. Elk (in herds of a thousand or more), antelope, mountain lions, wildcats, brown bears, and grizzlies were systematically destroyed by the farmers, ranchers, and hunters who came to the area. Settlers recalled seeing waterfowl so numerous that ducks flew over the bay in clouds thick enough to darken the sun.

"Everything fits. Every person, every creature . . . " But from where we sat, all traces of the gentle Miwoks had been erased, and only a few waterfowl could be seen.

Carol asked Easwaran if he thought it possible to reverse the deterioration of life that had occurred during the past several decades.

"I must say I'm an incorrigible optimist," he answered quickly. "I can't help it. I see what glory lies within each human individual, and I can only believe that it can be harnessed and used. But we need to restore a higher image of the human being than we have. People have to be persuaded that they are more than just a five-foot-eight-inch bundle of physical needs, that they have the capacity for a much higher mode of living. As long as you are convinced that satisfaction can come only from outside yourself, you won't be able to say no to personal desires, and therefore you are *going* to be a threat to the environment."

Thanks to his grandmother, he said, he had grown up with "an inkling" that there was something beneath the surface of the human personality, something "beckoning," beyond what he could see. "This is what people miss today, though they may not realize it. Especially young people: they have no models, no higher inspiration, no hint even that there could be a higher purpose to life than personal satisfaction."

"But do you think that educated, sometimes cynical, young people can even believe in a higher reality now?"

"Actually," he said, "I find that most people don't doubt the existence of a higher Self so much as they doubt the average person's ability to discover it. 'All right,' they tell me, 'the divine spark is within. You say it can be

experienced. But how many people can know it?' That's
what people often ask me."

"What do you tell them?"

He smiled. "I can only answer that any person with the
same determination as I had can discover the Self. I had
my share of problems; I made my share of mistakes. I was
born with all the natural urges of the average human
being, yet . . . "

He paused. "I know it can be done."

Easwaran looked as if he would like to linger a while
longer. Carol had started to put away her notepad and pen,
but now she pulled them back out of her jacket pocket.

"Easwaran, if this is a good time, I wonder if you'd mind
talking again about what finally brought you to the spiritual
life."

For a moment he didn't answer. A gust of wind blew
across the spit. "At one time or another," he said, "I had
probably imagined myself becoming any number of things
– a professor, a writer. I once had ideas of entering the foreign
service. But as a young man I don't think I ever had
the slightest suspicion that I would become a spiritual
teacher – or, for that matter, even take to the spiritual life.
I was energetic and ambitious, and I was aware of no
inner vacuum. I honestly believed I would be happy
with my success. Then the ground beneath me shifted."

"Could you say about when that was?" Carol asked.

"Yes. It was during the period following India's independence,
in the late forties. I began to feel that something
was missing from my life, but I had no clear sense of what
it was." With his intellectual's perspective, he said, he
could not have known that within his consciousness
"there was an undeniable need to know who I really was."

The more he struggled, the more this need asserted itself.
"I felt as though I were drowning. I grabbed for twigs

everywhere to keep from sinking – work, art, friendships,
entertainment – but every twig snapped in my fingers."
He quoted the medieval German mystic Meister Eckhart,
who described God as a "divine fisherman," looking for
people like him to catch. "I can easily imagine God," he
said, "standing waist-deep in the surf – right here! – wearing those boots that come up to the hips, casting his line
out into the waves. He catches something. It struggles.
And the more the fish fights against the hook, as Eckhart
says, the deeper the hook goes in."

Easwaran paused a moment. "If I had been a religious
person, it would have made more sense." He said that
after he left for college, he never went to the temple. Orthodox worship didn't interest him. "The world of literature and ideas was the real world to me." But the reality
of that world, he said, was being undermined by an "un-
explainable hunger." He tried to carry on as though
nothing were happening, but that only seemed to make
matters worse.

One night, he went to dinner at the home of a senior
colleague to whom his friend Naimuddin had introduced
him: a distinguished professor of Persian who was well
versed in Sufi mysticism. Easwaran had been made welcome in this home for some time, and the host's three
young daughters had all studied English literature under
him. Indeed, although the women of the family observed
strict purdah, the girls set their veils aside on the evenings
when they served dinner to Easwaran – a token not only of
the intimacy he enjoyed with the family but also of the
particularly tender relationship that can exist between student and teacher in India.

Easwaran's host had by now had ample opportunity
to observe him – had noted his one-pointed attention, his
passionate nature, and his innocence. They shared a deep
interest in poetry.

After dinner the men went outside with their host to sit under the stars and catch the light breeze. Naimuddin had just received an invitation to study and teach Urdu and Persian at the University of Ankara in Turkey. Easwaran, happy with his friend's success, was teasing him affectionately: "How is it that this simple fellow gets such a great opportunity, while I, with my sophisticated YMCA background, stagnate here in this out-of-the-way town?" But the older professor cut right through the playful talk. "Easwaran Sahib," he said in all seriousness, "I see the signs. It may be that the mantle of the mystic is going to fall on you."

This was not what the aspiring young academic had expected to hear from his senior colleague. "I panicked," Easwaran said. "I loved my work. I had students to teach, books to write, volumes with which to enrich the body of India's literature." The pronouncement threw him into an agony. "I lay awake all night, asking myself, 'There are four hundred million people in India – why should this happen to *me?*'

"My resistance was based on a universal misunderstanding of what spirituality means. I imagined my body being bent with asceticism, my senses suffocated with mortification, my life deprived of health, happiness, color, and friendship."

He soon forgot his friend's prophecy, but the deep restlessness persisted.

"Did you think about asking your grandmother?"

"You know, I was so intellectually oriented then, and she never used to talk much, anyway. And although I knew I loved her with all my heart, I had not yet even begun to grasp her real stature. She was always there, supporting me from within, but the understanding – that I had to arrive at on my own."

And so he followed his instincts: he read every relevant

book he could find. He steeped himself in Western psychology and attended lectures by intellectuals and writers of renown. "But they couldn't answer my most fundamental question: What is the purpose of life?" He began to suspect that regardless of their brilliance or talent, these thinkers had not discovered the meaning he was trying to find. "I would sit outside my circle of friends at gatherings, listening to the talk – talk I would have relished earlier. But now it all appeared so insubstantial, so impractical. I was thunderstruck at how frivolous we all were. I listened mostly to writers, because writing was my field. But they didn't have anything to say about these most fundamental questions."

He reached what he calls an "astonishing" conclusion: "The answer to my dilemma could not be found in books. They had only brought me more questions, while my discomfort grew. I had reached the end of my tether, and with no place left to go, I turned within."

He stopped talking a moment, long enough for Carol to ask him why, without apparent outside prompting, he had looked inside himself.

"That's the most puzzling part of all," he said with a look of bewilderment. "I can't adequately answer it, even to myself. What did make me decide to look within for answers?" He explained that these same questions occur to most sensitive people at some point in life. Usually, though, they despair, or become cynical or indifferent. Only a few make the decision to follow the hint that life is giving them and plunge within themselves. He repeated that he had never been a religious person, despite his grandmother's influence. He knew a number of people who had led far more "spiritual" lives, who seemed much better prepared for his fate than he.

"What made *me* decide to look within? I can only fall back upon my Hindu background for an explanation. I have come to the conclusion that it came about simply because of what the Indian tradition calls *gurukripa,* the grace of the teacher. My grandmother wanted this, and she got it. I have looked back over those decades carefully, and even now the only explanation I can offer is that I owe all of this to one person, my grandmother, and to the inestimable gifts she gave me."

Carol asked if he would elaborate on what he had called his grandmother's "gifts."

He spoke tentatively at first. "There was, of course, her boundless love. I always knew that she loved me far more than herself. This belief was rooted in my consciousness, and perhaps more than anything else, her love formed me. But that alone would not have been enough. She gave me something else . . .

"My grandmother was not afraid of death. She understood death. She knew it not as an end but as a passage." She knew this, he explained, not with an intellectual grasp but experientially, in the depths of her consciousness.

"In one corner of our home," he said, "was a room that no one entered – or entered only with reluctance. The children called it the 'dark room.' We were terrified of it. It was the room in which, following a death in the family, the corpse was laid before cremation. An oil lamp was set next to the body, and someone had to see that the flame was kept lit." This was village India, where superstitions about the dead were rife and profound, and no one wanted the task. "But my grandmother always volunteered, and she even slept there overnight just to make sure that the flame did not go out. She did it all with a sense of untroubled calm that astonished everyone." He himself asked her once how she could bear to spend a night with a dead body, and she laughed. "I am just sitting with a jacket," she told him. "That is all the body is. The jacket was old, and it has been taken off. What is there to fear?"

Chapter Three

"Did she pass on her fearlessness of death to you?"

"She gave me something much more valuable – she made certain that I would discover for myself that the body is only a jacket.

"In my village," he explained, "there was not the isolation from the drama of death that you have in this country. Here, death is hidden from view as much as possible, and the dead body is given over to professionals to prepare for burial, out of sight." It was different in his village, he told us. There, people died in the presence of their family and friends, whose grief added to the agony of the dying. "It could go on for hours, for days," he said. Each death was deeply felt because the families had intermingled for generations. "Each death palpably diminished our lives. We couldn't escape its significance. Even when we were young, death walked with us.

"As my grandmother's grandson, I had a special relationship to death – she saw to it – a relationship I only now understand. She made sure that I would not take death for granted by bringing me along when she went to give solace to a dying person or a grieving family. In that way I witnessed death many times, even before I had reached my teens, and sometimes in a terrifying form. Sometimes the screams of the dying person came to haunt my sleep." No one understood why his grandmother did this, certainly not Easwaran himself. Its effect was to sear into his consciousness a tangible sense of the reality of death.

It was her greatest gift, he told us. "My grandmother had seen to it that I would be forced by my knowledge of death's reality to come finally to terms with it. She knew I could never find peace or fulfillment until I had found out her secret: that death is *not* the end. This is the realization that lies at the culmination of the spiritual journey – a journey that begins only when we ask, from the depths of our heart, How can we go beyond death? This is what finally moved me to look within myself, and it was she who, in her astonishing wisdom, planted the seed of that discovery before I was out of my teens.

"There were many precious gifts my grandmother gave to me, but of them all, this was the most precious. She set me on the path to overcome death. Only a great soul can grant such a boon."

"And yet," asked Carol, "she never put this into words?"

"For her," Easwaran said, "life centered in the awareness of God was as natural as breathing. How could she explain the obvious to me? At a deep level," he added, "she knew what I was going through, knew that I would have to experience success and disenchantment. Despite my questions, she knew that I wasn't ready to hear the answers her life was giving me all the time. We have a saying in Kerala that you should never harvest green bananas. You must wait until they are ready, or you may damage them irretrievably. She knew I was still unready; I needed time. She couldn't give me the answers before I had formulated the questions out of my own experience. But she also knew that when these questions would finally raise themselves in my consciousness, the foundation for finding their answers would have been laid. She knew that because she had laid it herself."

When the ground did begin to shift under Easwaran, when not all the books he could lay his hands on could give him answers to his questions about life's meaning, he began to reflect on his grandmother's life. He thought about her character, her love and strength. "As I remembered all these scenes of self-forgetfulness and courage, I began to sense the scale of her achievement. She had been so natural about it all that I hadn't really taken note before." He began to understand that his grandmother had what he was seeking: security, peace, fearlessness, understanding, and "the limitless capacity to face life's challenges." His grandmother's indifference to death, he said, began to reveal itself for what it was: a continuous awareness of God.

He began to perceive her differently from before. "Perhaps my grandmother – uneducated and simple as she was – nonetheless knew what all these books did not know. My attention had been on Shakespeare and Dickens and the 'Ode to a Nightingale,' and I hadn't heard what her life was proclaiming every instant: that, as Blessed Angela of Foligno said, 'the whole world is full of God.'"

Now he began to hear. "I reached the rather embarrassing conclusion – after all, I was an intellectual – that my unlettered grandmother knew more about the meaning of life and its essential purpose than all the writers and philosophers I had been reading. Her whole life pointed in one direction – that happiness and fulfillment can be found only in awareness of God.

"I finally came to the conclusion that what I was looking for was not in books; it was not outside me. It was within. Half my life had been spent going away from my grandmother, but when I started to go back to her again, my life began to fall into place."

3

The clouds had drifted inland, leaving the sky over the bay a transparent blue. Easwaran stood up, pulled his gloves from his pocket, and slipped them on. Six pelicans glided overhead toward the sea. The large birds flew in a three-stroke choreography – beat, beat, beat, glide – like dancers in a ballet. Catching the light off the water, their wings looked almost incandescent. Easwaran watched them float by, then turned to look back at the three pelicans still perched on the landing. "Such ungainly creatures," he said. "You wouldn't think such grace was in them."

He took Christine's hand and they started walking fast, with quick, purposeful steps, arms swinging wide. Some long-legged curlews swarmed in front of us, then fell behind as we passed, probing the sand for food with their long bills. Along the beach lay bits and pieces of refuse half-buried in the sand: candy wrappers, a child's white sandal, pieces of sponge, a can of insect spray, bottles and cans and numberless aluminum flip-top tabs. What will archaeologists think, I wondered, a few millennia from now, unearthing bottle caps and antacid bottles along with the polished abalone beads of the Miwoks from a century or two before? Who had the better of things?

On our right, through the dunes, we could see the hill spotted now with the vivid forms of hang gliders – magenta, electric blue, tangerine: weekend fliers trudging up the sandy slope under their bright loads.

We passed a few strollers, a middle-aged couple napping near the dunes, a fisherman shivering in the waves (the water temperature here is often as low as fifty-five degrees), and a shiny Labrador pup flicking foam from his oversized paws. ("Only two creatures know how to use a beach," I remembered Easwaran saying another time: "dogs and children.")

Halfway up the beach, six teenagers stood in a huddle, scuffing the sand with their bare feet. They were looking down at something, and as we approached we saw that it was an immature harbor seal that lay just above the water line. It was panting heavily, its eyes wide open. Easwaran stopped and looked down at it. The trembling pup turned its eyes toward him, too weak to retreat. Carefully, Easwaran knelt on the sand and began to stroke the unresisting, doglike head, running his gloved hand back and forth over its damp fur. The seal did not turn away.

Chapter Three

The teenagers watched with cautious interest. One of them was tall and slender, with quick, serious eyes and a headful of blond hair that moved with the breeze. He stepped forward from the group, then dropped to his knees beside the seal. He looked into its eyes, then looked long and steadily at the man who was stroking it.

Easwaran didn't look up but continued to stroke the seal's small, pointed head. For some time the pup lay still, its wide, dark eyes fixed on Easwaran. Finally, the eyes dimmed and turned lusterless.

Easwaran turned to the boy.

The boy asked, "Is it dead?"

"His *body* is dead," said Easwaran, standing up and brushing the sand from his knees.

"You mean . . . ?" The boy glanced at the group of friends standing nearby, then back at Easwaran, who smiled warmly at him. Encouraged, he stood up slowly and asked, "Did you see how that seal looked at you?"

"Perhaps he knew I was his friend," Easwaran answered.

The boy pushed the long hair out of his eyes and paused again. He appeared to be struggling to frame another question.

Easwaran waited, unhurried. His seriousness matched the boy's own – softened, though, by the transparent affection that young people always elicit in him. He returned the gaze of the young man who was asking him, wordlessly, what the death of the seal pup *meant*. "It means that this same thing will happen to all of us," Easwaran said quietly, anticipating him. "To me, to you, to your friends here." He looked at the faces of the others, who stood watching with patient incomprehension. Then he turned back to the young man beside him. "But it will not be the end. Not for any of us."

Not a muscle moved in the young man's face, but the

look of struggle was gone. His gaze was eager now, and searching.

Easwaran clapped him on the shoulder, gave him another smile, and said good-bye. Then, waving to the others, he took Christine's hand and started up the beach. Had the boy been a few years older, I guessed, Easwaran might have let himself be drawn out a little more. Later he confirmed my guess, recalling his favorite Upanishad, the Katha, in which a teenage boy boldly demands answers about the meaning of death from a sage who is as fierce as he is wise. "Teenagers can show tremendous spiritual potential," Easwaran said. "They have the passion, the desire, the idealism, the reckless daring to stake everything they have on an almost impossible goal. But these young people need time, you know. My way is terribly demanding. Before they take on meditation and these other disciplines, they need every opportunity to explore all the innocent pleasures of life – and they need to begin to see through them, too!" Still, he added, if the young man on the beach were to turn up at one of his Tuesday night talks, he wouldn't be surprised. "I would be more than happy to see him."

More than happy. Spiritual teachers in the Indian tradition keep ceaseless watch for that special light in the eye of the most gifted students – the glint of gold. When the teenage hero of the Katha has passed the tests placed before him by the teacher and proven himself worthy of spiritual instruction, the crusty sage breaks into an uncharacteristic smile: "Blessed are you, Nachiketa!" he exults. "May we find more spiritual seekers like you!"

We continued up the beach, which was crowded now with people and their seaside equipment: blankets, radios, Frisbees, bottles of sunscreen, bags of potato chips. With the breeze behind them, Christine and Easwaran moved effortlessly over the packed sand. Undoubtedly, they were again repeating their mantram: the same mantram that Easwaran's grandmother had sung every morning before sunrise as she swept the open veranda of their home – the first words he would hear as he was awakening. It is a mantram, but it is a prayer too, uniting within it the legendary names of India's beloved incarnation-heroes: Rama, the warrior-king, and Krishna, the playful cowherd-prince, Easwaran's *ishta*, his Beloved Boss. This morning, I imagined, it might have served Easwaran as a prayer, offered to ease, and perhaps assist in its passage, the seal pup lying at the edge of the sea:

> *Haré Rama, Haré Rama,*
> *Rama Rama, Haré Haré,*
> *Haré Krishna, Haré Krishna,*
> *Krishna Krishna, Haré Haré*

Giving class in Berkeley, 1968

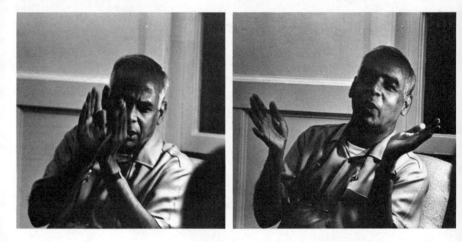

On a lecture tour in southern California, 1960

At the University of California at Berkeley, 1968

Berkeley, 1969

With niece Meera, 1971

4 | *Berkeley*
Flower and Fruit

1

*F*rom behind a flickering grillwork of metal girders high above San Francisco Bay, we look into a cloudless sky toward the city of Saint Francis. It is a spacious view, unbroken but for the long streamer of fog that has unfurled through the narrows of the Golden Gate and lies across the water beneath us.

We are crossing the Richmond–San Rafael Bridge, and Berkeley is our destination. Easwaran sits in the passenger seat, dressed in a gray suit and matching beret, and looks out across the scene: gray-green water, some islands of rock and wind-blackened grass, the Bay Bridge in the distance, and the ridge of hills that runs behind the Berkeley campus of the University of California.

A university man to the marrow, Easwaran moved to rural Marin County nearly twenty years ago, but he has never lost his affection for the charmed, contentious enclave of students and scholars on the east side of the bay, where he lived and worked for almost a decade during the formative years of his Blue Mountain Center.

Today he has tickets to a play by George Bernard Shaw presented by the university's drama department. We've brought a picnic dinner from home, but before we eat, there will be time for a stop in Berkeley and a walk on the campus. Tonight's itinerary is a favorite of his. Other evenings might take him to the Berkeley Repertory Theater, or to Zellerbach Hall on campus to watch a folk-dancing ensemble from Greece or a mime troupe from Czechoslovakia.

Easwaran always takes a few friends along on these occasions. Outings to Berkeley or San Francisco are all in a day's work for him, providing contact with his closest friends that is more intimate and sustained than the daily round of ashram life affords. For Easwaran the spiritual teacher, the dinners and plays are much more than recreation: "I'm on duty all the twenty-four hours," he claims, only half in jest. "Christmas, Easter, Hanukkah – even Halloween!"

Now, the station wagon is fragrant with the aroma of the spanakopita baked for our picnic dinner, wrapped in towels to keep it warm. A tossed green salad and a bowl of cut-up fruit are packed in an ice chest along with a bottle of mineral water. Fresh-squeezed orange juice (to mix with the mineral water) will be bought along the way. We glide down the slope of the bridge toward the sprawling flatlands of Richmond while the bay and its cities unfold beyond us. Over the water, the fog sparkles under the bright sun.

Easwaran watches the scene silently, his shoes off, his legs crossed underneath him on the seat. No one is talking. The windows are closed, and only a murmur of noise reaches us from the engine. Outside, there is surprisingly little traffic; within, a sense of peace and well-being. It has little to do with what is outside and much to do with Easwaran himself. From his presence there can issue a peace that is almost palpable, and I feel it again now as I drive – a difficult feeling to describe, yet unmistakable in its effect. I recognize it in the words of Saint Catherine of Genoa, words which Easwaran has quoted often: "*And the state of this soul is then a feeling of such utter peace and tranquility that it seems to her that her heart, and her bodily being, and all both within and without, is immersed in an ocean of utmost peace. . . .*" Saint Catherine's words resound in my mind, and I almost say them aloud but think better of it. Easwaran himself silently watches the water and the cities beyond . . .

Our first stop is Monterey Market, produce capital of the East Bay. The parking lot is jammed, and shopping carts are at a premium. Inside, the aisles are crowded with people of every race and nationality, the shelves and bins with produce of every sort. Lotus roots and tomatillos, enoki mushrooms and fresh ginger, custard apples and long beans, four kinds of eggplant, bunched fresh herbs, round Japanese pears, gooseberries, blue corn: you can find the raw materials here for any cuisine – and half of Berkeley seems to have come looking. Lines for the check stand stretch almost the length of the building.

Easwaran's twenty-three-year-old niece is with us today, and they enter the market together. This is Meera's second prolonged visit to California; she lived here for three years as a child, then went back to India, returning to California three years ago as a junior in college. Now she is nearly finished with her master's degree in journalism. Two friends from her newswriting class will be meeting us later this evening, before the play: she's eager to introduce them to her illustrious uncle.

Holding Meera's hand, Easwaran walks the aisles with deliberation. This market is not simply a source of produce, he says, but a gallery for displaying the Lord's – his

"Boss's" – artistic talents. "It all reflects an artist's touch," he says, gazing at a flaming heap of red bell peppers, "a marvelous eye for color and form." In fact, in his Tuesday night talks he often compares Monterey Market to an art gallery. Now, stopping, touching, he takes it all in with barely subdued delight. "The Lord could have made everything square, for easy packing," he says, running his finger over a knobbed jicama root that looks like the footpad of a small elephant. "But he didn't."

"Uncle," Meera says, smiling, "they have ash melon today; let's get one for Auntie!"

It's a private joke. While Christine and Easwaran were living on the Blue Mountain, there were times between seasons when the only vegetable the marketplace offered was ash melon, a singularly flavorless gourd for which Christine conceived a deep weariness.

"We can spare her," he says, smiling back.

The aisles are packed now in a rush-hour traffic that nears gridlock at the cash registers. Small children ride the shopping carts, whooping over the voices of checkers (surely some of the world's fastest) calling out prices in Japanese; two African men converse in French; several older women lament the price of asparagus in pure Brooklynese. A considerable din, a drumming, marketplace clatter. But right now Easwaran seems unaware. He stands oblivious to it all, his attention riveted on a shelf where Meera has spotted the season's first mangoes. Easwaran eyes the orange-gold fruit – a childhood passion – with cautious interest. This is May. It is too early for mangoes, and Easwaran is a prudent man. But he is a hopeful man as well. He lifts two mangoes in his open palms, weighing them in some invisible balance. He sniffs the skins, presses their tips with his thumb, then sets them back in the bin. "Another week," he says. "Perhaps."

They are more fortunate where fresh coconuts are con-

cerned. Easwaran notices a new shipment on the other
side of the market, and the two of them edge through the
noisy, packed aisle in front of the check stands. Easwaran
takes his time, seeming to savor the rich variety of faces
and languages.

When they reach the bin, they both look over the coconuts, which are large and promising. Meera shakes
several judiciously, listens, and selects four.

They are an arresting pair. Meera is every inch an
Eknath, straight and slender, quietly self-possessed, with
large, dark eyes and a beautiful smile. Easwaran takes
great delight in her company; it is clear that when she is
with him, something of his mother and grandmother are
there too.

At the campus we are met by Michael, a classics professor, and Julia, who is a student in the English department.
(Both live at the ashram.) We carry our fragrant cargo up to
an empty departmental lounge, where Easwaran will dine
with us. First, though, we'll all stroll across the campus.

Outside, maples, sycamores, and a wide, rolling lawn
shape the landscape to our left; redwoods and a creek extend to the right. Straight ahead are the granite steps of the
Life Sciences Building, where Easwaran gave a course on
meditation during the sixties. He surprises us now by
starting up the steps.

He has a strong sense of history (he says that in this regard he is very un-Indian) which occasionally draws him
back to the places where he began his work: the house on
Walnut Street in Berkeley which became the first home of
the Blue Mountain Center of Meditation, or the Tilden
Room on campus, where he gave the noontime talks that
attracted so many of the people living with him today.
Room 2000 LSB is one of those key places, yet it is not nos-
talgia, I think, that draws him back here this afternoon,

but gratitude – and a certain wonderment. "Remember," he says as we enter, "it all started here."

LSB is massive and neoclassical, girded with fluted columns and copper-framed windows. At the end of a long hallway, we find the door to room 2000, an auditorium which for many years housed the largest natural science lectures. Below us, the floor slopes downward to a long, black demonstration table with several water and gas taps. From behind it have lectured some of the world's foremost scientists.

On the evening of Monday, January 3, 1968, 2000 LSB had standing room only for the several hundred Berkeley students who had registered for The Theory and Practice of Meditation (Religious Studies 138X, four units' credit; instructor, Eknath Easwaran). To anyone's knowledge, it was the first accredited course on meditation offered by any university in the United States – or, for that matter, in the world. An article on meditation in a national weekly described Easwaran's course, mistakenly referring to the Blue Mountain Center of Zen Meditation. For ten Monday nights, Easwaran sat atop the black veneer of the demonstration table and lectured on the ancient mystical teachings of the Indian spiritual tradition. Required texts included Patanjali's Yoga Sutras, the Upanishads, the Bhagavad Gita, and Sidney Spencer's *Mysticism in World Religion.*

Students were given instructions in meditation during the first class and were asked to meditate thirty minutes a day throughout the course. Easwaran also asked them to record their observations in a meditation journal, which served as a laboratory "log" for the observable effects of the experiment that they were performing, as he put it, "on the mind, with the mind, by the mind." One student wrote, "This class is so fantastic, and you get four units of

credit for taking it. Can you imagine this happening anywhere but Berkeley?"

Half an hour of meditation followed the lecture. The
lights would be dimmed, and hundreds of enterprising
Berkeley students would lay aside their notebooks, settle
themselves in their chairs, heads and backs erect, close
their eyes, and focus their minds on the world-shaking
words of the poor, luminous saint of Assisi: "Where
there is hatred, let me sow love . . . "

2

"Those were marvelous classes," Easwaran
said softly, surveying the large, high-ceilinged room. "Any
spiritual teacher would have loved to have those students:
thoughtful, energetic, restless – a perfect combination. It's
wonderful to think that hundreds of such eager students
came here week after week, all wanting to learn about
meditation and the spiritual life."

"These things come in waves," he added, "and I suspect
that we are just at the beginning of another one that may
even surpass the sixties. There is a need in the human
heart for meaning, an overriding spiritual drive that has to
assert itself eventually. We can block it, hide it, deny it –
and we all do! – but there comes a time when it cannot be
appeased any longer."

He looked up at the blackboard – a new one: triple-
tiered and double-width, with an acre of writing surface.
A lecturer had written a list of key terms for his students:
*growth and repro, nucleus, DNA, memb bound, mitochon-
dria, chloroplasts, limit of resolution.*

"It's just a matter of time," he murmured.

As we were leaving, two students, book bags over their
shoulders, passed us and turned back to stare at Easwaran.

Chapter Four

"They probably think you're Satyajit Ray," I said after they walked by. "He's on the campus this week."

"I've been mistaken for him before," Easwaran replied, smiling. "I've been mistaken for a lot of surprising people in Berkeley. Satyajit Ray I can understand. Even Krishna-murti. But I thought it a bit thick when some fellow mis-took me for John Gielgud."

He quickened his pace for a few minutes' serious walk-ing, then we headed back toward the lounge, where our picnic dinner was waiting.

Posters and bulletins papered the hallway leading back to the lounge: *The College Year in Scandinavia. Workshop in Tantric Meditation Techniques. U.C. Karate Club. Spain, the Land of Romance.* Easwaran took a moment to look them over. "Not much has changed since I was a student – certainly not human desire. At that age, I was enchanted by names like Kalamazoo and *Champs-Elysées.* The allure of foreign lands. Somewhere else. *Anywhere* else!" He walked on down the hall. Four students came toward us, an animated knot of them, talking in French – all four at once.

"I never get tired of watching the faces of students," he told us as we entered the lounge. "The ones I see here are just like the ones I knew in India. So fresh, so eager to learn. So innocent and idealistic."

Bells sounded across the courtyard from the campanile just up the hill – Vivaldi: a spirited send-off for weary stu-dents and professors leaving the campus, but deafening at close range. We closed the lounge windows.

Easwaran took a place at the table, and the rest of us joined him. Framed prints by European masters hung on the walls behind us: Titian, Velázquez, and Goya. Julia slid wedges of spanakopita onto paper plates; Meera mixed the mineral water and orange juice. Easwaran closed his eyes. Vivaldi and the whir of commuter traffic pressed through the closed window as we all silently repeated our mantram.

While we ate, Easwaran asked for all the campus news: a faculty petition was circulating that protested the university's connection with a weapons research laboratory, Michael said. Julia mentioned that it had become difficult for a student to find an affordable apartment in Berkeley. On one of the bulletin boards she'd seen, a student had posted an index card offering five hundred dollars as a "finder's fee."

Someone pointed out that enrollment of minority students had increased so much that no one ethnic group formed a majority on campus: as of last fall, the combined enrollment of Asian, Chicano/Latino, and black students made up more than fifty percent of the total. Easwaran greeted this last bit of news with visible pleasure. His own university campus in central India had drawn students from all over India and from all of India's religious traditions. The diversity itself was no small part of the education, he believed.

The conversation turned to Easwaran's earliest days in Berkeley, as a Fulbright scholar in 1960. He'd been housed in a hotel on Telegraph Avenue just off campus, he told us, and found himself directly above the busy street. Its clatter made meditation almost impossible, so he went down to the desk on his first morning to request a different room. "I was very inexperienced in those days," he said. "I just walked up to the man at the desk. 'I say,' I told him. 'I meditate.' I expected him to understand that I needed a quiet room. But he didn't know what to make of it. Finally he asked me if I needed some special equipment!"

"It was like that in those days," he said. "Most people had no idea what meditation was. Not even in Berkeley. One morning one of my students was meditating in his car and a policeman stopped to ask him what he was doing. He told him he was meditating. The policeman looked puzzled, then finally asked, 'Do you need any help?'"

For a few minutes we ate in silence, then Carol said, "You couldn't have found it very easy to be a vegetarian when you came here."

"No. Sometimes I just had to go hungry. Even on the campus, I could hardly find anything vegetarian to eat. I would walk through the entire cafeteria line and end up by the cash register with nothing on my tray. In those days, I ate a *lot* of ice cream."

He had finished his spanakopita and was halfway through his salad when he put down his fork. "You see, I feel very deeply for all these young people coming to the university. They have so much to contend with – the housing shortage, drugs, violence. It seems unfair. Worst of all, perhaps, they come here in hopes of finding answers to their questions about life. And all they hear is that happiness means having money, prestige, power. It's no wonder that they become disillusioned. These things *cannot* satisfy their deepest needs.

"They need the kind of beacon which only ideals greater than oneself can give. Otherwise their natural sense of idealism finds no outlet, and they feel stifled and don't know why. Then they indulge in all kinds of self-destructive activities, and that's when the trouble starts. To my eyes, these are merely signs of increasing spiritual restlessness. These young people today don't know it, but many of them have simply reached the end of the material tether."

Carol mentioned that students at a local junior college had formed a meditation club. "They're very serious," she told Easwaran, "and in many ways they're more mature than we were at that age. By the time they get out of high school, they've seen a lot more of life than we had – and they aren't easily taken in."

Easwaran listened thoughtfully. "What I want to bring out above all," he said, "is that now I see my life as a trust. And I see the lives of everyone around me in the same light. My time, my energy, the health of this body, all these are a sacred trust now – I can use them all for serving life. When I walk on the beach, when I eat asparagus or spinach for dinner, I do it because I want to live a long, long time carrying on this work.

"And this is what I hope to help these young, eager, bright-faced students to understand too: that their energy, their intelligence, their artistic talents are all a trust. There is a place for it all – all of life stands in need of what they can give, and it is the university's role and duty to nurture all this youthful energy. Their talent and all their gifts need to be drawn out and developed for the benefit of everyone."

I asked whether he'd thought about particular ways in which the university might do this, and he nodded vigorously.

"You know, for example, that we are in the first stage of a terrible ecological crisis. The consequences of industrialization and careless use of resources are bearing down on us all. You can view this as a disaster, but there is a bright side to it too. It means that there is good, meaningful work for every one of us."

3

The sky outside was nearly black when we finished dinner. We opened the windows. Traffic was down to a murmur; the bells were silent. We cleared the table and packed the plates and bowls into wicker carryalls. In a while we would walk to a coffeehouse near the campus where Meera's friends would be waiting, but in the meantime, it was clear that Easwaran was more than willing to continue our conversation. He sat on the sofa and invited our questions.

His mood was so serious and searching that it seemed an appropriate time to ask a question that we'd raised before but he had answered only sketchily. Would he explain to us exactly when and how he had begun to meditate? And how had he hit upon his own particular method of meditation?

"Very well." He said he would explain as best he could. He began slowly. "I told you that I had already reached a stage when I had become completely disenchanted with life. I knew that the answer was somewhere within me. But I did not yet know just how to find it." His disenchantment with life, he said, magnified his long-felt sense of life's transiency. "I had become haunted by how ephemeral life seemed," he told us. "Even as a boy, probably because of my grandmother's influence, I had been struck by how quickly the flowers wilted and died, how relentlessly life around me altered."

As a graduate student, he lost a friend to typhoid. "He was a good-humored, likable fellow, quite a clown without being clownish, and a good musician. We both caught typhoid, but one day he just died. I attended his funeral and wondered why he had died and I had not. His death must have shaken me deeply. Do you remember what Larry in *The Razor's Edge* says when he looks at the body of his comrade? 'The dead look so dead when they are dead.' I must have been affected like Larry, at a deep level. I wasn't ready to turn inward at that time, but my friend's death left its mark."

Then there had been the Second World War and, in India, famine. Following the war, India was partitioned, and thousands of people were senselessly killed in communal rioting. All this forced on him an acute awareness of the fragility of life, especially of the suffering it brings to creatures.

"Were you at all aware of the underlying unity then?" one of us asked.

"I must have had an inkling of it," he said, "but I wouldn't have called it by that name. Being aware of the unity of life means that you feel very intensely the pain of others, and I certainly felt that. At first you just get an inkling, something you can't quite put your finger on. You feel a continuous discomfort, a sense of wrong that somehow has to be made right, but you don't quite know what to do." He said that the pain can become so intense that it can hurtle a person onto the spiritual path without his even knowing it.

"That must have happened to me. That would explain why suddenly, for no apparent reason, everything I had held meaningful in life turned to ashes. I couldn't make the connection. It was a terrible time for me," he said. "The values I had cherished, the ambitions I had followed for years suddenly meant nothing to me. I simply couldn't abide the seeming senselessness of life any longer, its dreadful frailty."

And there was his own aging. "After all," he said with a smile, "I had reached the halfway point in life. There were a few wrinkles, and there was some loss of hair – and among those that chose to remain, a few were gray. 'So,' I thought, 'It's going to happen to me too.' Oh, I tried for a while to pretend it wasn't taking place, as everyone else does. I even bought some Brylcreem for my hair. But the evidence was too vivid. Time was passing. Death – though I was healthy and vigorous – was nonetheless approaching. I began to feel that I was in a kind of race between myself and time, between myself and death."

"What did you do?"

He laughed. "I didn't *know* what to do. By now the bomb had burst in my consciousness. I had to find out if there was something beyond decay and suffering and death, something that did not change and die. It became a frantic search for me. I couldn't get it out of my thoughts, or even my dreams."

He stopped a moment. "It was not the desire for goodness or even happiness that made me begin to meditate. I had to find a way out of time. As I said, I knew that the answer, if there was one, was within me, but I didn't know how to go about finding it. Now, some unseen force unleashed by my grandmother just picked me up and set me on the path to find the answer. She had shown me that I would have to find the solution to my problems within myself, but she had left it to me to find the way.

"When grace descends upon you like that, the first thing you lose is your peace of mind. I was willing to try anything reasonable to regain it, but I couldn't find anyone to show me how. 'Breathe love thoughts to the Divine,' someone told me. 'Become one with the Supreme.' Even then I knew this sort of thing was mostly pious talk that – as the British would have put it – buttered very few parsnips. I wanted to find out the meaning of death. Nothing less."

Carol asked, "Do you remember when you actually started meditating?"

"It was a gradual process," Easwaran said, "and an almost natural one." He explained that he already had highly developed powers of concentration, and his work on the campus kept him absorbed. "I could get lost in my work, but when I came home, the aimlessness of life – its dreadful impermanence – would start to oppress me. It troubled my sleep greatly. I reached a point at which I just couldn't see any sense anywhere. Many nights, I couldn't sleep at all.

"There is one occasion in particular that you could call
a watershed. I was on my campus in central India – was in
the classroom, teaching, in fact – when I received from my
Uncle Appa the telegram that told me my grandmother
was passing away. 'Don't come,' it insisted. My grandmother knew it would be too much for me to bear.

"My mother was at my granny's side, of course, and
an exchange took place which I learned about only much
later.

"'What will I do without you?' my mother had cried.
'I'll be alone – I cannot go on living.' And my grandmother
answered, 'Never say that. You will see. I have made a
mountain of your boy.'"

In years to come, she would understand. But at the
time she was inconsolable. Easwaran abided by his grandmother's request and did not go home until summer vacation. He found his mother devastated by the loss.

"They had been mother and daughter, sister and sister,
friend and friend for decades. When I saw her then, I knew
I had to do something. She would not have survived long."

He remembered the Nilgiris, the Blue Mountains,
about seventy-five miles to the northwest, and sensed that
the cool climate and English country setting could help
restore her spirits. Before she quite knew what was happening, he had rented a small cottage in the town of Ooty
and begun looking for a permanent home for them. "We
arrived at night, so we couldn't look around the neighbor-
hood. The next morning I walked out of our cottage and
found a Ramakrishna mission next door. It was hard not
to see this as auguring well!"

Within a few weeks, he had found a bungalow in a
nearby town, bought it, and moved his mother in. It was
indeed an auspicious move, for his mother soon recovered
her resilience and lived another thirty-three years. For
Easwaran, it proved just as beneficial. The high, quiet

hills, sixty-five hundred feet above the dusty plains, provided a healing respite from campus life. Each year for a decade he returned to spend the summer months with his mother.

"While she was living there we had two dogs, German shepherds, that I had raised from pups. They were deeply attached to me, and I to them. I would take them on walks with me. They were vegetarians. When I would return for summer vacation after nine months on my campus, one of them would actually get so overcome with joy that she would come close to having seizures. At the end of the summer, days before I left to return to the campus, she would come and lay her head on my feet. When it finally came time for me to leave, she would let out a dreadful howl that almost broke my heart."

One day, Easwaran returned from a walk to learn that this dog had been killed by a passing car. "My mother was as concerned about me as she was for the dog. She knew how fond I was of it. I didn't know what to do. I was heartbroken. Almost instinctively I went to my room, picked up my Gita, and began to recite the verses to myself. My grief must have been so great, my need for consolation so deep, that I was quickly carried far into my consciousness, and I found that somehow my sorrow had been transmuted. I had gained some vague understanding that my dog would go on, that this was not the end. This deep comfort confirmed my sense that meditating on these verses could help me greatly in my search for the answer to suffering and death. I began to suspect that I had found a way to peace."

"Had your grandmother taught you to meditate on a passage?"

"No," he said. "I had to figure that out for myself. My grandmother didn't need to learn to meditate because she came into this life already knowing how; she was always aware of God."

At night when he couldn't sleep, he recalled, he took to silently reciting passages from the Bhagavad Gita. They brought him some consolation and peace of mind. And more: "I discovered that when I opened my eyes, an hour or two would have gone by without my knowing it. And I would be left with a prepossessing sense of peace that would follow me into the day, into my work. *'What is this?'* I wondered."

"Why did you use a passage?" Carol asked him. "Wouldn't most Indians have meditated on a mantram?"

"I was intellectually oriented. I had grown up in the world of books. I don't think that the mantram alone would have helped me then. These verses spoke directly to my condition. A few lines, a phrase repeated at those depths – *'You were never born; therefore you will never die'* – and the whole sky would light up with meaning For a time the darkness around me would vanish and my sense of a deeper self would expand. I began to suspect that there was indeed a force inside me, a presence other than my own small ego.

"I don't remember thinking about posture or anything; it just came about naturally. Before long, at the campus, I began to get up at five – not because I knew it was the best time to meditate, but because I had to be in class. It was all so natural, so effortless. I can explain it only within the Hindu and Buddhist background of reincarnation. I must have learned all of this in an earlier life; I can't think of any other explanation. Before I knew where I was, I had gone far into consciousness."

"How did you start practicing the other steps you teach, like sense training and putting others first? Did those come as naturally as meditation?"

"Not quite as naturally." He laughed. "After all, I had developed my share of questionable habits. But I saw myself in a footrace with death, so you might say I went into training. I changed all my eating habits, for instance. As my inner life intensified, I sensed almost intuitively that there was a natural balance to be maintained, so I began to take regular, vigorous walks for exercise. I began to juggle with my likes and dislikes. Much of this was under the influence of Gandhi. Every week I would scour the pages of his little journal for tips on nutrition."

"How soon did you begin to notice changes in yourself?"

"Surprisingly soon," he said, "I found that I could face some of my deepest fears and resolve them. I could transform my negative urges. You know, I couldn't believe the impact my behavior was starting to have on those around me. My students, and even a few of my colleagues, began to seek me out for help. This confirmed for me that the peace and strength I felt inside was not a hallucination. It had its effect on the external world, even without my conscious knowing. I understood that I was not meditating just for myself. I was developing the capacity to help others find security as well.

"My development was very rapid," he added. "Perhaps, in retrospect, too rapid. It caused me a lot of suffering. In deep meditation, many changes occur in your nervous system, in your sleeping habits. They can cause a lot of discomfort. I went to several people for advice, but they couldn't give me any help. One of them was a good monk who had been meditating for some decades. I explained my experiences, and he just put his hand on my shoulder and said, 'You've been blessed.'"

"So you carried on without a teacher to guide you? Entirely on your own?"

"Alone, but not without guidance. My grandmother had

shed her body, yes, but she had not left me. One night
I found myself in deep waters in meditation and felt as
though I were sinking fast. For some reason, I began to
sense my grandmother seated by my side. She comforted
me, protected me, and, as she had done a thousand times
when I was a boy, pulled me out of trouble. My grandmother was not dead, I realized. I began to call upon her
strength to overcome my fears. I felt protected, supported."

He paused. "You see, as I've said before, when a person
becomes aware of God, he or she is no longer just a person,
but a living force. My grandmother did not die; she merely
shed her body. She was – she *is* – very much alive in me. I
don't think I understood this until that night. But once I
did, I knew that I was in her hands – that I always had been
in her hands – and that there was nothing to fear. She has
protected and comforted me ever since."

"Did you ever reach a point where it seemed hopeless
. . . impossible?"

"No. But there were times when I doubted whether
I would ever reach the goal. Then I suffered terribly."

Someone asked if he would describe them.

He did not speak for some time. Perhaps he was searching for words to describe experiences that were essentially
inexpressible.

"There were times in the deeper stages," he said,
"when I would fight for months to change levels of consciousness. Great leaps have to be made then in the depths
of the unconscious, and I just couldn't make them." He
paused. "It is almost impossible to describe this state. Do
you remember Tarzan in the movies, swinging from tree
to tree on a vine? It was something like that, trying to
swing from one level of consciousness to the next and not
being able to make it to the next tree." He could swing far
out on one vine, but could not let go of it to catch hold of

the next one. "It was terrifying," he said. Each time, he swung back to where he had started. "I might have even touched the branch of the next tree," he said, "but I just couldn't let go of the first one. And letting go is essential!"

This went on for weeks, months. "It became almost unbearable," he said with some emotion in his voice. "Two hours of meditation, two hours of trying to reach the next level, only to fail, again and again. I began to think I was never going to make it. And the thought cut my heart into pieces. To come so far and not to reach the goal – which I now *knew* was real – I found almost unendurable."

"But you succeeded."

For a moment he didn't answer. "I think I told you earlier that I had always wanted to be like my grandmother."

"You said you wanted to share her fearlessness," I said.

"Yes, and now, when I reached this stage in meditation, I found I was more like her than I had suspected. Many times I was tempted to say, 'What's the use?' But the prospect that I would fail turned me into a raging animal, just waiting to pounce on the next meditation. No matter how black things looked, I would not give up. I dreaded each meditation, but I looked forward to it too.

"To put it differently, it was as though I had come up against a great door, like the fortress gates they built in ancient India. They have huge spikes protruding in front to protect the fortress against elephant charges. To fall against that door caused a lot of pain. But no matter how hard I tried, I just couldn't break through. I even dreaded sitting down in meditation, knowing that the door was there and that no matter what I did, I could not break it down. It is at this time that people who have come far along the spiritual path can give up. I knew of a few of them myself."

But Easwaran would not be denied. Signs appeared that he was nearing the goal. The door began to give. "My

grandmother just would not let me give up," he told us.
"I kept at it, day after day, month after month, throwing
myself against that door." Through effort, through sheer
spiritual agility, through his grandmother's grace, the
leaps were made. "I kept trying. And one day the door
opened and I was flung inside."

I asked if he could describe the experience.

"Not very well. I had reached a stage so deep in the
personal unconscious that the physical world became a
dim memory, and separate life a distant dream. I saw light
everywhere. It was unutterably beautiful, beyond words to
describe. When I came up from meditation, I found that
the physical world of separateness was still very much in-
tact, and darkness still reigned as before. But inside, the
lamp had been lit – rekindled, I should say. Some time
later I read a description of this experience by Saint Teresa
of Avila. She called it 'the light without a night.'"

Easwaran has always been cautionary about spiritual
"phenomena" – visions, sounds, internal movements.
"Seeing a light within," he said flatly, "is not sufficient evidence of spiritual progress. The light I saw was not a passing, momentary phenomenon. It was followed by a permanent change in my consciousness and behavior."

"Can you tell us about that change?" I asked.

"What is the time?" he asked. It was all right; we had a
few minutes.

He explained that "all kinds" of inhibitions and fears
had fallen away, fears coming from far below the surface
level of consciousness. He had struggled with them for
years, with little success. Now he found that he could
enter the areas of consciousness where those fears lurked.
"I found I could just pick them up," he said, "and throw
them out. I was amazed at first – it really worked! – they
were gone for good." He said he felt as if ropes had been
untied from within. "My hands and legs were free, even

though I hadn't known they were bound. I recalled that one of the Gita's descriptions of the illumined person was *abhaya*, fearless. This is one of the predictable fruits of meditation."

"*Just* meditation?"

"It was the result of years of discipline, years of meditating and training my senses carefully and trying to put others' needs first. All of this was necessary. After all, one does not simply sit down on a meditation pillow one morning, see a flash, and then find a roomful of old inhibitions and fears lying about."

I asked if there were other areas of his life that had changed as dramatically.

"Many," he answered. He found that he could make reversals in his likes and dislikes: with food, with opinions, even with people whom he had disliked. "A kind of spiritual perversity came over me," he explained. He began to court people with whom he did not get along. "Especially colleagues who disagreed with my opinions." He could become friends with them, he found, even though they might continue to disagree. It gave him an extraordinary measure of freedom.

"Oh, so many discoveries came in those days," he said, "that it was as if walls were falling down everywhere in the unconscious. I realized I was developing mastery of the mind – conscious, subconscious, unconscious – all the way from the attic to the cellar. It meant that when a violent craving came up, I had the freedom to say, 'Hey, presto!' and the craving would go."

He stopped. The ringing of the campanile bells told us it was seven o'clock. The last note hung on the air as Easwaran continued. "The discoveries kept coming," he said, "week after week, year after year. I felt as though I were being carried along in the arms of my grandmother. The same arms that had brought me into this world were

now helping me into the next." He said that a time came
when he plunged completely within himself, into the
depths of the collective unconscious. "No words can describe this. At that time you are no longer in the world of
space; you are no longer in the world of time. The body
and the mind are left behind, and you discover the deepest
sources of your life, the deepest sources of your being. And
you enter into an eternal relationship with the Self, the
Lord of Love in the depths of consciousness, call it Sri
Krishna, the Christ, the Compassionate Buddha, or the
Divine Mother.

"You realize that you are not just a petty personality
but part of this divine unity. After that, death can hold
no terror, because death applies only to the body, and you
know that you are not your body. You understand in the
depths of your being that though the body will someday
have to be shed, your deepest Self will live always."

"What about the deaths of others; how do they affect
you?"

"As you well know, I grieve. Every month, it seems, I
receive news of the death of yet another member of my
ancestral family or someone with whom I grew up or went
to school. I feel the loss. It does grieve me terribly, but
despite my grief, I know it is not the end. I *know* this
without a doubt, in the deepest core of my consciousness,
and nothing can shake that understanding."

He stopped, looking as though he had finished. I had
hoped he would describe his state of mind during these
final stages of his spiritual journey. Fearing that another
opportunity would not arise – he had rarely talked about
these experiences – I decided to ask if he remembered how
he felt.

"Unworthy," he answered, his voice touched with
emotion. "I knew people who were far more spiritual than
I was, people who were more disciplined and had made far

fewer mistakes than I had made. And yet . . . I didn't understand then, and I don't understand now. I can only explain it in terms of my grandmother's grace. I have no other explanation.

"There is another wonderful passage by Saint Teresa of Avila in which she describes the ways that grace can come to the spiritual seeker. For some, she says, grace is like water that is drawn from a well – a bucket here, a bucket there. It takes lots of hard pulling even to get a few bucketfuls. For others, grace flows to them like water from an irrigation channel. The water pours from the river in a rush, but it takes a lot of hard digging first. But for some, Teresa says, a rare few, grace simply falls upon them like rain – falls freely, copiously upon them – bathing them."

He paused for a moment. "I still remember my unending joy during those times, when throughout the night I slept under just such a rain. I can think of no reason for this other than the grace of my teacher. Is there any way I can adequately express my gratitude?"

4 |

Easwaran's glance at Meera now assured her that he hadn't forgotten her friends. Briskly, he rose and pulled on the lightweight overcoat she held for him. Everyone picked up a basket or bag, and we were off.

Stopping briefly at the parking lot, we left our things in the car and walked to the coffeehouse where we were to meet Meera's friends. Pools of bright light flooded our path as we crossed Strawberry Creek and passed a grove of redwoods before emerging onto University Avenue. The fog glowed in the street lights, and the night air had a rich, woodsy fragrance.

It was just cool enough outside to enhance the pleasure of walking into the warmth and brightness of Upstart Crow, a bookstore cum cafe where the aroma of good coffee made the shelves and tables of books all the more alluring. We walked past the book displays to the back of the room, where a long table was being held for us.

The walls there were lined with photographs of twentieth-century literary figures. As we sat down, Easwaran recognized first a cherubic Yeats, then a raffish G. B. Shaw. Carol pointed out photos of Virginia Woolf and James Joyce. Easwaran joked briefly with her about the one occasion when he had been required to teach something by Joyce and how at sea he had felt. With Shaw, though, it had been love at first reading.

"I admired him as much for the quality of his thinking as for his art," Easwaran said. "In fact, it was really Shaw who taught me how to think clearly. And he was one of the few great modern thinkers who lived what he believed."

He smiled. "In fact, on Shaw's ninetieth birthday – I was teaching by then – I sent him a congratulatory telegram in which I pointed out that he should realize he was truly world famous now because we were celebrating his birthday there in remotest central India!

"You know, he was a vegetarian, and this meant a great deal to us. All his doctor friends told him he couldn't possibly survive without meat; they truly believed that in those days. But Shaw lived to be ninety-four, and when someone suggested he go back to his medical friends and remind them of their earlier prognosis, he said he would love to, but they had all passed on!"

Meera's two friends arrived. She introduced them, and it turned out that they too had tickets to see *Major Barbara*, so we continued to talk about the great Irish playwright.

Someone remarked on the timeliness of the play's theme, and Easwaran concurred: "Shaw was an indefatigable opponent of war. I don't think peace activists today give him the credit he is due for helping change our thinking about war. He wrote a book criticizing British attitudes during the First World War, when it wasn't just an unpopular thing to do, but dangerous. He was called a traitor."

"Didn't Shaw meet Gandhi when he was in England?"

"Yes, when Gandhi attended the Round Table Conference in the thirties, he and Shaw met. I think he is said to have remarked later that Shaw was a very religious man who did not believe in God. That was a brilliant observation."

Between sips of decaf espresso, Easwaran drew Meera's friends out: What were their professional plans? What sort of writing did they want to do? He urged them not to be discouraged if their efforts weren't warmly received right away. He assured them that he had received many rejection notices before he was first published. "*De*jection notices," he called them, chuckling. "I could have carpeted my study with them."

He talked with them about the power of the media, pointing out that the focus on violent confrontation in newspapers and on television has diminished our faith in nonviolent solutions. "There is so much that people in your profession can do," he told them, "by bringing to our attention what is best and noblest in human nature. You know, our image of what the human being *is* has become so tarnished, so small."

They were all taking the same newswriting course, so Easwaran asked them what kind of stories they were working on. Shyly but eagerly they told him, and the conversation flowed effortlessly.

Such a blithe portrait – Easwaran chatting about literary loves, drinking his decaf, enjoying the sight of students leafing through books at nearby shelves. It was a little disorienting to recall that only half an hour before he had been describing to us his descent to the deepest levels of human consciousness.

Afterward, we walked a few blocks in the light mist to the campus theater for *Major Barbara*, which turned out to be a lively, competent production. Easwaran especially enjoys student performances, and he allows a wide margin for inexperience. Tonight's performance, though, needed no margin. Shaw's quirky, insightful humor sparkled through beautifully, as fresh and topical as ever; and the students, Easwaran remarked as we were leaving, had acted at a near-professional level. A kind of afterglow lingered in the car as we drove out of Berkeley and back toward the bridge.

. . . Now, stillness, as we cross the bridge above the bay, encapsulated in night and a thick ocean fog. The wet air glows under the lights of the bridge, and as I drive I can see nothing of the bay or the cities beyond it. A peace has settled on us, and on the faintly glowing night. Everyone is silent, probably meditating. In the dense quiet, I hear only the tires on the damp pavement and the *tok, tok* of the windshield wipers clearing away the drizzle.

As it had this afternoon, the sense of peace and well-being in the car has become almost palpable. I steal a glance at Easwaran, the center of it all. He has his eyes closed, hands folded in his lap. As we start down the far slope of the bridge, a gust of wind shreds the fog in front of us, revealing bright patterns of light from the cities beyond the bay, and above them, against the darkness, sharp points of starlight. Easwaran remains still.

> . . . *and all both within and without, is immersed in an ocean of utmost peace.* . . . *And she is so full of peace that though she press her nerves, her flesh, her bones, no other thing comes forth from them than peace.*

At work, about 1976

At work, 1988

With Christine at Ramagiri, 1988

With niece Meera, 1988

With a young friend, 1988

5 | Petaluma
A Teacher at Work

The church where Easwaran gives his Tuesday night talks sits on top of a hill that commands an expansive view of the entire Petaluma River basin, all the way east to the Sonoma hills. Built in the 1950s, when family churchgoing was at a peak, the church is good sized. Its sanctuary can accommodate more than two hundred, not counting the choir loft, and the parking lot is large.

This is fortunate, because in the past couple of years Easwaran's talks have been drawing near-capacity crowds, despite the fact that they are not advertised anywhere. Regularly, someone from Petaluma or a town close by will turn up who is just a little exasperated: "I've lived here ten years," he or she will complain, "and I only found out yesterday that he speaks right here in town! Do you have to be so discreet?" Perhaps not, but the advantages are real. People who find their way here are usually well prepared: either they've read at least one of Easwaran's books and called Nilgiri Press to find out where he talks, or they have heard about him from a friend, relative, or co-worker.

This Tuesday evening, the fellowship room is open as well as the sanctuary. Every couple of months, particularly on the Tuesdays following retreat weekends, when many guests from the retreat are still in the area, there is a coffee hour before class. People bring cookies or fresh fruit and spend the time getting to know one another. When the weather is clear, as it is this evening, the gathering spills out onto the patio and lawn just outside.

Probably thirty of the people in attendance tonight have been at last weekend's retreat and have extended their stay in order to see Easwaran just once more before returning to Louisville, or Seattle, or New York City. Earlier this evening, in fact, the room was just beginning to fill up when there was a flurry at the door. A woman from Denver who had come to the retreat and had presumably left on Monday walked in, grinning broadly. Her husband was just behind her. "Hey, I thought you had gone!" someone said to him.

"Well, it was close!" he said. "We were scheduled to fly out yesterday. I tried to change our reservations to tomorrow, but couldn't get a flight. We were already on the plane and buckled in when a flight attendant announced that the flight had been overbooked. He asked if anybody would be willing to fly out tomorrow. Diane was up and halfway down the aisle before the guy had stopped talking!"

A friend of theirs from Boulder walked up, surprised, and heard their story. "Great! I'll be on the same flight." The Denver constituency, we call them – the ten or fifteen people from the Denver-Boulder area who come regularly to these retreats and meet weekly in one another's homes to meditate together and listen to Easwaran's tapes. Similar groups have formed in twenty cities across the country.

We're making heavy use of the church's facilities tonight. In the upstairs loft, fifteen people are having their regular weekly meeting. This is Hasti, the adult counterpart to Friends of Wildlife.

Hasti is one of the many Sanskrit words for "elephant." Literally, it means "long arm" (referring to an elephant's trunk), but Easwaran chose it as a name for the group to imply the expansive reach he hopes it will have in rebuilding the environment – for both elephants and ourselves. In fact, Hasti's members have been surprised by the effect they are beginning to have on national and international environmental policy. Their main strategy comes straight from Easwaran: personal contact and gentle persuasion aimed at helping opponents in a conflict realize that they are all on the same side, while the problem – be it poaching in Africa, inappropriate handling of American zoo elephants, or dwindling wild habitat in Asia – is on the other.

Tonight Hasti is meeting to determine its position in a controversy that has recently reached the California legislature regarding the treatment of elephants in zoos. Hasti is a young organization – just four years old – but its fair-minded and resourceful approach has already won it a good hearing. Its members played a part last year in relocating a zoo elephant who might otherwise have been destroyed to a new home in a New Jersey zoo.

Hasti's is not the only departure from a strictly sociable format. In the sanctuary itself, three or four people have their heads together over a proposed design for a book cover, and in another corner, four RISE group leaders are meeting.

It's a lively scene, and Easwaran appears to be enjoying it immensely. To conserve his voice, he doesn't usually speak much during the hour before class, but his presence is very much felt as he walks about. He has stopped in at the Hasti meeting for a while and answered some questions about how elephants are trained in South India. He has also made a special point of spending a few minutes with people who will be leaving tomorrow. Now, though, he is standing quietly with Christine. He is smiling, his gaze resting on a cluster of high school and college students just outside. There has been a dramatic increase in the number of young people attending these talks in the past two years. At first, when there were only a few of them, they looked a little shy and self-conscious. But now that their numbers have grown, they seem perfectly at home. Their presence at Easwaran's talks has made a difference that can be felt even when reading a transcript of the talk later. Their liveliness brings out a corresponding vitality in him – and a rich vein of humor.

The crowd around the coffee and herbal tea urns is thinning out, and everyone is moving toward the sanctuary, where Easwaran will speak. Barring illness, which is rare, Easwaran gives these talks every Tuesday night without fail. Christmas, New Year's Eve, the Fourth of July – there are no exceptions. He is all the more committed to holiday evenings, knowing how many people are alone at those times. Now, he ascends the steps to the platform and sits down. His expression is serious but relaxed. His gaze travels around the room while a microphone is clipped to his jacket. He takes a sip from the stainless steel cup on the table beside him and once again begins to speak, just as he has each Tuesday night for a quarter of a century.

"The Bhagavad Gita can be looked upon as an artist's manual – a living manual for all who wish to make their life a flawless work of art. When you are looking at a painting by Rembrandt, there is a certain satisfaction – but it is only for that moment, and it is only for yourself. When your whole life becomes a masterpiece, though, everyone around you benefits.

"Tonight, we will look at the last eighteen verses of the Gita's second chapter, which Mahatma Gandhi called 'the summit of human wisdom.' The first verse is a question. 'Tell me, Lord Krishna, of the man or woman who is established in wisdom: How does he sit, how does she stand, how move about?' In other words, 'How can we recognize him or her?' The Sanskrit word for 'established,' *stitha*, is cognate with *stand*. A mind that is 'stitha' is unwavering – unaffected by praise or blame, by rises or falls in fortune. It was by becoming the embodiment of *stitha prajna* that Gandhi was able to make an artistic masterpiece of his own life.

"A mind that is steady," Easwaran explains, "a mind that has been trained not to leap or plunge with every impulse of pleasure or pain, is no longer subject to depression." With unarguable simplicity, palms upturned, he adds, "A mind that goes up *must* come down. If you pursue excitement, you are signing up for depression too."

By easy steps, he gradually widens the application of that simple term "established in wisdom." If we are dependent on praise, for example, we will inevitably fall apart when we receive criticism. He recalls reading about a Hollywood film star so addicted to adulation that he went to sleep to the sound of an applause machine. "But you see," he says, as the laughter subsides, "we *all* have our applause machine, right there in the mind, playing back what our boss said about our work that morning, what our professor wrote on our essay, what our girlfriend said on the telephone. Unfortunately, life doesn't always throw roses. It throws brickbats too, and bad tomatoes. One day, roses – next day, bad tomatoes! And if our peace of mind requires roses, the bad tomato days are going to be unbearable."

Easwaran's hands are narrow and tapering, and he uses them to remarkable effect as he speaks. Most of the classical dance forms in India involve beautifully expressive gestures called *mudras*, and certain of Easwaran's gestures bring those to mind. Yet they are quite his own, and so economic, so understated, that one usually isn't even aware of them. They support his meaning, or lend ironic weight, but never call attention to themselves.

"It is the nature of the mind," he continues, "to be restless, turbulent, always on the lookout for something it can attach itself to – for pleasure, for security, for self-aggrandizement. This has nothing to do with morality; these are just the dynamics of the mind. It doesn't *want* to be made steady. It welcomes distractions. And the mind's henchmen, or secretaries, to use politer language, are the senses. For it is through the senses that most distractions come."

In a moment he will supply the Gita's solution, but first, he prepares us.

"Years ago, when my niece Meera was small, Christine and I used to take her, with her sister, Geetha, and my mother, to a small zoo in Marin County. The first time we went there, we were surprised to see an enormous tortoise walking about the place as if he owned it. On his back was painted a sign: 'Don't report me. I'm free!' My mother was delighted because it reminded her of the tortoises we used to see in Kerala. Particularly when it has rained, they will come out on the path, and for schoolchildren this is a great treat. They run up to the tortoise with little sticks and tap him on the back as if he were a kind of drum. As soon as the tortoise sees children coming, it tells its limbs, 'Withdraw!'"

Suddenly, and for just a split second, Easwaran *is* a tortoise, head pulled into his high Indian collar, arms and legs tucked in close. "As soon as it even hears the school bell, the tortoise says to his limbs, 'Get in, and stay in!' The children can play the drums all they like then; the tortoise is unaffected."

He grows serious again. "This is the background against which Lord Krishna draws out his marvelous simile: 'As a tortoise draws in its limbs,' he tells us, 'you can train your senses so well that when danger approaches, you just say 'Withdraw' and they will – instantly. Then nobody can hurt you; life cannot victimize you.

"When you are able to do this," Easwaran promises, pausing, "*All* compulsive behavior falls away. Drinking, drugging, smoking, overeating – from all of these, like the tortoise at the zoo, you are free."

Over the years, countless men and women have expressed their gratitude to Easwaran for his approach to addictions of one kind and another. He is absolutely nonjudgmental. "This is a come-as-you-are party," he maintains. "I've never asked anyone to give up drugs and *then* meditate, or to stop drinking and *then* come to class. Take to meditation, start practicing the other disciplines, and see whether, *gradually*, the need for drugs or the craving for alcohol does not finally abandon you altogether."

But when he is talking about compulsive forms of behavior, he goes well beyond those that are commonly seen as addictions, such as alcoholism or drug dependence. Gently, with enormous humor and compassion, he extends his analysis to include, for instance, strong likes and dislikes and attachment to one's own opinions. "You should be able to lay your opinion out in a discussion and see what happens to it," he says tonight. "If it ends up crumpled, torn, and illegible, leave it – it probably wasn't worth keeping. But if it holds up well under attack, like one of those plastic credit cards you can't destroy if your life depends on it, fine; you may have an opinion worth keeping."

Recreational shopping comes up next, as he describes a

newly opened luxury shopping center in San Francisco that he visited recently. "I must say, these people know how to manipulate us. I felt as if I were in a cathedral, or a great temple. The floors are paved in marble. There are no clocks, and a new perfume called Eternity was given a big display. A poster proclaimed the secret of our identity: 'Born to shop!' There was a kind of artificial light – like the one Wordsworth describes, 'never seen on land or sea' – and it gave everything an unearthly glow. No expense had been spared.

"Perhaps the only disappointment was the men's room," he added with a smile. "It had not been paved in marble, and that did strike me as a sad lack . . . "

On other evenings, he might talk about how many hours people watch television and what they see, or gambling, or chronic anger, or the habit of procrastination. The touch is always light, the comic element never overlooked. Yet finally, everyone's private demon – petty or monstrous, singular or plural – comes up for inspection. And in every case he demonstrates that there is only *one* demon: a mind that is out of control. He concedes that a trained mind is a tall order. Yet . . .

"Through these marvelous disciplines – by following them carefully and enthusiastically – I have become able to tell my mind just what to think, and when. If I don't want it to think, I can turn the ignition off, put my key in my pocket, and give my mind a wonderful rest; then, when I need to think, all I have to do is turn the key and start the engine." The room is silent and expectant.

"This may seem impossible, but many of you have been watching the Olympics this week as I have, and you have *seen* that on the physical plane the impossible can be achieved.

"What is the Olympic slogan? '*Citius – Altius – Fortius:* Faster – Higher – Stronger.' Every four years there are athletes who break the world records established in the previous Olympics, pushing past all the presumed limits of the human being to do so. And as I watch, it all unfolds as a perfect metaphor for the magnificent adventure of Self-realization."

Easwaran cannot always count on the common frame of reference he has tonight, and he makes the very most of it. Very likely, all but a few have watched the Olympic Games – thrilled at the unbelievable speed of the tiny California swimmer Janet Evans, the stunning grace of the Romanian gymnasts, and the quiet, determined heroism of diver Greg Louganis.

"A few days ago," Easwaran says, "while diving, Greg Louganis hit his head on the springboard. He could have been seriously injured – four stitches had to be given. But he didn't say, 'This hurts terribly – I'm going to bed. America can send somebody else!' Thirty minutes later he was back, and he won the gold medal. See, that is the spirit. The same spirit is required in meditation. The deeper you go, the more difficult and the more dangerous it will become."

Drive, determination, and a good coach: "People ask me sometimes, 'Why should we have a teacher for meditation?' I say, look at what has happened to American gymnasts since the Romanian coach who trained Nadia Comaneci came to this country. Bela Karolyi can bring out the very best a student is capable of, and this is what a good teacher of meditation can do."

Easwaran has been moved by the extreme youth of this year's athletes. He is stirred deeply by the intense concentration in their eyes as they stand poised at poolside or crouched at the starting line. "It's a perfect setting," he says, "for the all-out recklessness of the teenager."

And as a man of letters, he is endlessly amused by the technical vocabulary associated with each event. He enjoys teasing out his own meanings from terms such as "love all" and "dropping your shots" in tennis or the "false start" of racing events. He savors the comic inscrutability of phrases like "clean and jerk," which weight lifters employ. Today he has been watching the volleyball finals, and a fresh string of terms has fired his imagination.

"The three critical skills," he tells us, "appear to be 'blocking,' 'digging,' and 'killing,' but it was the first one that really caught my admiration. The American player would jump high and pound the ball straight downward with all his force, and suddenly there would be a Dutch player directly under it, hands right against the ball. It was like a thunderclap when the ball struck his arms, and another when a great roar of applause followed."

Again, he leans forward for emphasis. "This is just what happens when you resist a fierce desire. There is such joy in that, you know. Suppose you have a very strong craving for something that is bad for your body. You block it! There is such freedom in this. When there is a healthy drive, you yield to it, of course. But when it is an unhealthy drive, a selfish drive, a conditioned drive, jump and block.

"And when the player has successfully blocked the ball, all the team members run about like this" – he mimed the "high five" with both hands. "It's just like that in your body when you resist one of those powerful desires: all your nerves applaud; all the muscles say 'Bravo!' You feel energy rising. All the cells in your body rejoice."

And how does one *block?*

"Breathtakingly simple!" he says. "But it takes training – long, hard, persistent work – before it *becomes* simple. When you have a craving, just keep repeating your mantram. These desires have deep roots in the conscious and preconscious levels, but the mantram can go even deeper if you've been repeating it at every opportunity. It can get under the desire and 'dig,' to use again the language of volleyball.

"When we first gave our meditation class on the Berkeley campus, one of the students wrote in her meditation journal, 'I dreamt I was sitting at my favorite ice cream parlor, about to eat a huge ice cream sundae.' She actually named the place and said that this particular dish was called 'The Nightmare.' 'But when I was just about to plunge in my spoon, I heard the mantram and the whole bowl was tossed onto the floor.' I gave her an A for the course!

"You see, none of these problems starts out big. They start with such little things. You visit a bakery, someone points out a special pastry, you try it, and . . . *not bad.* A few days later you come again. Same thing. After a few weeks, as soon as you walk in, the proprietor smiles and asks, 'The usual?' Slowly it becomes a habit; then the habit gradually becomes a compulsion, and finally, an addiction. When this has happened, it is terribly difficult to change your behavior. But what meditation can do, over a long period, is first to shrink the addiction into a compulsion, then the compulsion into a habit, and finally – you are free. You sit up and rub your wrists and ankles, and you realize: the chains are gone. The compulsion is gone. Then a tremendous amount of energy flows back into your life, because a lot of energy is trapped in compulsive desires."

If he were to stop at this point, no one, I think, would feel deprived – it is such a supremely empowering image of ourselves he has given us. But he goes on, in the same ebullient, optimistic tone, to matters of grave global importance.

"I want to go back now to the question we began with: 'Tell me of the illumined man or woman. How does he sit, stand, move about?' I would like to extend that and ask, 'How does the man or woman who has become aware of

God relate to the universe? How does he treat the air, the water, the forests, and the topsoil?' We know now that what becomes of the environment bears directly on our own health, and the health of our children and *their* children.

"The Gita's position is precise and utterly practical: You and I own nothing on the face of the earth. Everything is owned by the Lord. We are all trustees who are expected to take good care of Mother Earth, who is, in the Indian tradition, a living goddess. If we pollute the air and the water, if we cut down rain forests and wash away topsoil, we are hurting our mother. And in doing that, we are destroying what belongs to our children and grandchildren. 'Here,' we are saying to generations to come – 'here is Mother Earth, stripped of the topsoil that should have grown your food, her waters unfit to drink, her air unfit to breathe, the forests gone where wild animals roamed and birds sang.'

"If we are to reverse these suicidal trends, we must immediately start to question the assumptions of a consumer society and adopt a simpler, less destructive style of living. Every one of us can do this, in a hundred small ways. Let me suggest a few."

Easwaran reads widely to keep abreast of the major issues of our time. Hardly a talk passes now when he does not touch on some facet of the environmental crisis that is overtaking the world today. Tonight's talk is no exception.

"Fifteen miles above the surface of the earth, between us and the deadly ultraviolet rays of the sun, the Lord in his infinite mercy has placed a thin layer of ozone. It is absurdly thin, yet it is all that stands between us and skin cancer – all that protects the plankton in the sea, the microorganisms in our soil, from assured destruction.

"We are learning now that the chlorofluorocarbons used in air conditioning, in refrigeration, in industrial solvents, and in manufacturing the ubiquitous Styrofoam cups that litter our beaches and streets are destroying that protective shield.

"To halt the damage that has already been done, a great many measures will have to be taken, and some will require considerable scientific expertise. But the city of Berkeley has taken a simple and immediate step by banning the Styrofoam cup."

Easwaran lifted his stainless steel cup for all to see. "I carry *this* wherever I go because I have banned Styrofoam personally – and I urge all of you to do the same. If each of you can just determine right now that you will forgo Styrofoam cups and containers, you'll have made a loving, restorative gesture toward our mother, the earth. Little, little things, you see, but all of us can do them, and they add up.

"Take another example, something that the media are bringing to our attention right now – the so-called greenhouse effect. During the past hundred years, we have used up half the fossil fuels that have formed over the course of four hundred million years. And as we do so, we are producing forty thousand tons of carbon dioxide each *minute*. As the amount of carbon dioxide in the atmosphere increases, so does the temperature.

"If our use of fossil fuels continues at the present rate, the temperature will rise sixteen degrees Fahrenheit by the end of the next century. Ice caps will melt; our beautiful beaches will disappear; fertile fields will become dust bowls: all this will happen during our children's and grandchildren's lifetime."

The picture is dark – yet Easwaran's perspective is invariably optimistic. As always, he reminds us how much we *can* do.

"You and I can reverse these trends in the little choices we make every day. For instance, we don't have to buy things we don't need – like disposable Styrofoam cups – just because someone else wants to manufacture them! If we don't buy, they won't make!

"And we can decrease our use of fossil fuels by reconsidering all the trips we make in our car, too. We can walk, we can bicycle, we can carpool. You know, each day twenty thousand cars enter San Francisco with only one occupant. Traffic would be cut by ten thousand cars if each of those drivers took along just one other person.

"There is more – and this is something our children can join us in doing. We can plant trees. Trees are our natural first line of defense against the greenhouse effect. They breathe in carbon dioxide, retain the carbon, and release life-giving oxygen into the atmosphere. According to the journal of the American Forestry Association, we have one hundred *million* spaces appropriate for planting new trees around our homes and communities.

"A dozen trees planted by every family will ensure that our children and grandchildren will have pure air. It's as simple as that – a great gift we can give them, and we don't have to wait for Christmas! I am not against buying cars when necessary, but when you buy a new car, plant a dozen trees around the garage. In fact, if I were the president of an auto company, I would insist: 'Have you planted your trees, Sanford? Have you, Claudia? Then you get your car. If not, come back when you have.'

"And I would add one more suggestion. Once you understand the vital protective role played by trees, it becomes clear that when tropical rain forests are destroyed, it is an assault on the lungs of Mother Earth. There again, we are not helpless. One of the primary reasons the rain forests of South America are being destroyed is to provide grazing land for beef cattle to provide hamburgers for the United States. If we go vegetarian, and encourage others to do so, we can prevent their destruction."

He has been speaking of the most overwhelming, pervasive threats of our time and making us feel that they can be met – met, ultimately, in the same way he has told us our personal problems can be solved – by making choices in areas where we thought we *had* no choice. It is the fine art of the possible.

In conclusion, he returns to the Gita.

"Whichever country we come from, whatever race we belong to, in the depths of our consciousness there is a living spirit which can be discovered. That is the purpose of life. We have to undergo difficult disciplines to make this discovery, but when we do, our body glows with health. Our energy becomes endless; our decision making becomes flawless – and our relationships grow richer and richer.

"Through the blessing of my grandmother, I don't have to close my eyes to see that living spirit. I see it everywhere, disguised as men, as women, as children, as beasts of the field and birds of the air. Everybody has become my brother or sister. Equally important, the mountains and the rivers, the forests and the fields have all become part of my family.

"In the language of the mystical tradition, we have very little time on earth. Even a hundred years is a short time. The man or woman of God will not spend one day idly, not one day uselessly. Such people understand that all of life is a trust – the air, the seas, the soil, the forests. Their actions will embody this understanding, and this is how you will recognize them."